Taking Learning to Task

Taking Learning to Task

Creative Strategies for Teaching Adults

Jane Vella

JOSSEY-BASS
A Wiley Company
San Francisco

Published by

JOSSEY-BASS
A Wiley Company
350 Sansome St.
San Francisco, CA 94104

www.josseybass.com

Jossey-Bass books and products are available through most bookstores. To contact Jossey-Bass directly, call (888) 378-2537, fax to (800) 605-2665, or visit our website at www.josseybass.com.

Substantial discounts on bulk quantities of Jossey-Bass books are available to corporations, professional associations, and other organizations. For details and discount information, contact the special sales department at Jossey-Bass.

We at Jossey-Bass strive to use the most environmentally sensitive paper stocks available to us. Our publications are printed on acid-free recycled stock whenever possible, and our paper always meets or exceeds minimum GPO and EPA requirements.

Library of Congress Cataloging-in-Publication Data

Vella, Jane Kathryn, 1931–
   Taking learning to task : creative strategies for teaching adults / Jane Vella.
      p.   cm.   (The Jossey-Bass higher and adult education series)
   Includes bibliographical references and index.
   ISBN 0-7879-5227-3 (alk. paper)
   1. Adult learning.   2. Adult education.   3. Learning strategies.   I. Title.
II. Series.
LC5225.L42 V43 2000
374/.13 21
                                                        00-008333

FIRST EDITION
HB Printing   10 9 8 7 6 5 4 3 2

The Jossey-Bass Higher and Adult Education Series

Contents

Tables and Exhibits

To the memory of
Paulo Freire and Malcolm Knowles,
founders of the feast

Preface

Socrates knew it. Jesus knew it. The Buddha knew it. Every open question asked as the peripatetic crowd in white togas strolled around Athens, every parable put to the crowds at the lakeside, every subtle image set for unraveling in the heat of India was a learning task. These great teachers set great learning tasks because they knew the power of dialogue.

African youth in their cohort, facing a challenging route to manhood, are given a set of demanding learning tasks. Astronauts who are facing an inviting universe move through a grueling set of learning tasks. A new mother, apprehensive and humble with her infant in her arms, faces a daunting daily set of learning tasks.

What Is a Learning Task?

A learning task is a way to structure dialogue. It is an open question put to members of a small group, who have been given all the resources they need to respond. A learning task is a way of ensuring engagement of learners with the new content. Structuring dialogue by setting useful learning tasks is one way to effective teaching. It took me a long time, I confess, to move from writing teaching tasks in my lesson plans to designing learning tasks. When I prepared teaching tasks, I was not inviting dialogue. I was structuring my monologue.

It is taking me an even longer time to transform teaching into learning by being faithful to the learning tasks I design. As I heard Paulo Freire put it, "Only the student can identify the moment of the death of the professor." When I discovered that I was a learner as well as a teacher, I could identify the moment of death of the professor in me.

A common pattern of teaching has been for the professor to lay out the content (skills, knowledge, attitudes) and then design exercises so that learners work with what they have heard or seen in order to learn it. This pattern is not only what teachers expect to do. It is what learners expect as well.

In this book, we examine a different approach, where teaching and learning are integrated and where the learning task is the overall design, incorporating the lecture or input along with practice.

Goal and Objectives

In this book, you are challenged to describe the difference between teaching tasks and learning tasks. You examine both the theory and the practice of this approach to build useful skills. Once you have completed reading this book and doing the learning tasks, you will, I trust, think about using learning tasks as you design your courses, seminars, and workshops for adults. This is the goal of the book.

Notice that the goal is general. This book is designed as a series of learning tasks. Here are the specific achievement-based objectives:

By the time you finish this book, you will have

- Examined assumptions behind the use of learning tasks
- Defined a learning task as a way of structuring dialogue
- Explained the difference between teaching tasks and learning tasks
- Reviewed the seven steps of planning (Chapter Three) to see how these relate to learning tasks

- Identified the direct correlation between an achievement-based objective, a set of content, and a set of learning tasks

- Identified the differences among an inductive task, an input task, an implementation task, and an integration task

- Examined a list of verbs for discrete cognitive, affective, and psychomotor learning tasks

- Examined a checklist of principles and practices for leading learning tasks

- Identified three levels of questions for program design decisions: epistemological, categorical, and personal

- Distinguished between learning tasks and testing tasks

- Practiced designing learning tasks

- Reviewed evaluation components: learning, transfer, and impact

- Named connections between current adult learning theory and this approach of using learning tasks

We accomplish all this in twelve chapters. In Chapter One, we examine the assumptions and theories behind the use of learning tasks, and we propose a definition of a learning task. Chapter Two provides a descriptive distinction between teaching tasks and learning tasks. Chapter Three shows how a curriculum or a single course can be designed using the seven steps of planning to result in a set of learning tasks.

In Chapter Four, we look at four types of learning tasks: inductive work, input, implementation, and integration. Inductive work connects new learning to old; input involves lectures, readings, slide shows, and videos in presenting the new research and content; implementation tasks are those in which the learners do something with the input; and in integration they project or practice putting new content into their life and work. In Chapter Five, we examine verbs that work best in learning tasks. In Chapter Six, we use a checklist of principles and examine three levels of questions for program design.

Chapter Seven addresses the skills needed to lead learning tasks and to reach and teach diverse learners. Chapter Eight reflects on the issue of time and the learning task. In Chapter Nine, we see how this approach to learning can work with diverse topics.

Chapter Ten shows how learning tasks can be used with all types and cultures. Chapter Eleven describes using learning tasks on the Internet and for distance learning. Chapter Twelve is a synthesis chapter, offering a set of reasons and principles for the use of learning tasks.

Three Appendices offer examples of a program using learning tasks, selections from a distance-learning course using this approach, and a set of technical guides to designing and using learning tasks.

If you have read my earlier works—*Learning to Listen, Learning to Teach* (1994a), and *Training Through Dialogue* (1995)—you are familiar with using achievement-based objectives that lead to learning tasks. This book, like the earlier two, invites a new way of thinking about education. We speak now of a learning-centered approach to education; it puts *learning* at the center, not teaching, not the teacher, and not even the learner. It demands accountability of both the teacher and the adult learner. I urge all teachers in training, all graduate students in education, professors of education, and professors and students of training for global management to be prepared for the shock of this transformation. This is not a comfortable shift in perspective and practice. It takes courage to change how we teach.

This book is designed to be a practical guide to an epistemology for learning-centered teaching that considers adult learners as subjects or decision makers in their own learning. I propose that such an epistemology is the only appropriate one for a civil, global society that is based on inclusive democracy. We cannot invite men and women to take a moral stance if they have not been practicing it consistently in their learning. It is my hope that this book be used as a text in adult education courses around the world, to teach teachers at any level how to organize their teaching into learning-centered designs through the seven steps of planning and learning tasks. I imagine schools of education not only teaching adult educators how to teach this way, but actually teaching this way—folding their lectures into cogent, demanding learning tasks.

I trust this text will be challenging and useful to adult educators in any field. I urge you to watch the process within the book, noting how the material is arranged in sequenced learning tasks to engage and move you to learn as you read and work. Welcome to the practical world of learning tasks, where dialogue is structured into learning-centered teaching.

Raleigh, North Carolina   Jane Vella
April 2000

Acknowledgments

This book would not be in your hands without the encouragement and collaboration of those whom I think of as colleagues at Jossey-Bass, especially Gale Erlandson.

My friends and coworkers not only supported this effort but also offered excellent suggestions along the way. Professor Sarah Gravett in South Africa has taught me much of what you share in this book about the value of learning tasks.

The Author

Jane Vella has worked in education since 1953, when she taught a third-grade class in Spanish Harlem in New York City. Since then she has taught and studied in the field of community education in forty-two countries around the world.

Vella is the author of the Jossey-Bass publications *Learning to Listen, Learning to Teach*; *Training Through Dialogue*; and *How Do They Know They Know* and is a contributor to the recent volume *Spiritual Dimensions of Adult Learning*. In August 1999, she collaborated with Sarah Gravett in South Africa in writing a distance-learning course.

Vella is an adjunct professor at the School of Public Health of the University of North Carolina at Chapel Hill, and the CEO of Global Learning Partners, a consulting and training company that has grown out of JUBILEE Popular Education Center.

Taking Learning to Task

1

Learning Tasks: Assumptions and Definition

Learning Tasks 1 Through 4

A lawyer, Rosa Lee, came to me saying, "I know the laws and the processes of mediation I intend to teach, but I really do not know how to teach them."

For years, Lee had lectured her way through a thirty-hour course on mediation in high-cost divorce cases, teaching priests and ministers, lawyers and paralegal professionals how to use mediation techniques to keep couples out of law courts. The lectures and occasional role plays offered much information on the law and some practice in skill building, but they gave no assurance to her or her students that they knew what they needed to know. "How can I be more accountable?" she wisely asked.

Lee assumed that without her lectures the professionals she was teaching would not come to know the law. That was what her professors in law school had assumed. They lectured her, and thus she learned the law.

As we examined her assumptions together, she discovered that she believed the professionals she taught really did not have the capacity to enter this mediation process without hearing a great deal about the law regulating it. She believed in the lecture as the only instrument for presenting that information, and she assumed her responsibility was to organize her presentation and offer it to listening learners. Although Lee had gnawing questions about accountability, she understood it as her responsibility to present a comprehensive argument.

Lee and I worked through the seven step planning process (see Chapter Three) and designed a series of learning tasks for the professional participants to do during the thirty hours. Most of the learning tasks involved either reading or listening to her lecture on the topic, and then doing something with that new content.

Lee was surprised at the energetic response of learners to these learning tasks, and at her new role as mediator of learning. She observed small groups in heated argument over the implications of the law, in creative design of alternative questions to put to husbands and wives in the throes of a disputed divorce, and in hearty laughter at their own anecdotes of analogous situations.

She concluded that her assumptions about the group and the process needed redesign. In her words, "I see now that what I believe about the learners and about the learning process controls what I design, what I teach, and how much they learn."

Learning Task 1: Assumptions

As you read this section on assumptions, consider what the opposite of each assumption involves.

Learners Have the Capacity to Learn

Setting effective learning tasks takes humility. An associate of mine recently complained about how hard it was to sit for hours during a professional workshop while learners completed learning tasks in small groups. He had designed and set excellent learning tasks, the learners were clearly learning and collaborating in the learning, and the products were sharply defined indicators that good learning took place. Still, he complained about his new and apparently diminished role.

Granted, it would be so much more satisfying for him to tell them the meaning of what they are about to learn, and to describe to them in brilliant detail how significant the material is to their jobs and their lives. He would be happy to tell learners stories about other people learning this content. Their applause at the end of his teaching would be gratifying, indeed. No complaints would emerge about that.

It takes humility even to entertain the notion that a set of learners, adults or children, men or women, professionals or community folk, come to classes, workshops, or university courses with the capacity to learn as well as the capacity to listen. This is our first assumption: learners arrive with the capacity to do the work involved in learning.

This assumption relates to the psychological theory of projection. As a teacher, I look out on a group of adults or teenagers or children and what I see is largely determined by who I am. My assumptions about the capacity of learners to do the work needed to learn during the learning session are based on my perception of my own learning capability.

I trust that your reading this book is a healthy sign that you share this assumption about not only the capacity of the people you teach but your own capacity to learn.

There are, I suspect, few teachers today who do not hold that learning must be active, that learners must be engaged and held accountable for their learning. Why, then, does the huge gap persist between that common knowledge and the daily practice of adult education we experience in industry, academia, and the community?

Active Engagement in Learning

Our second assumption is that learners learn when they are actively engaged—cognitively, emotionally, and physically—with the content.

Such engagement can be cognitive, affective, or kinesthetic, depending on the content. It can be deeply reflective or fiercely argumentative. Engagement can begin with the lives and experience of the learners, or with the research-based new content. Although it can take on as many shapes as there are learners, it must be intentional and designed.

I think of my three-year-old neighbor. "Me do!" Peter insists, because he is relentless about taking every possible chance to learn. He is a tiny, energetic learning machine. "Me do!" "Me do!" Little Peter reminds me that we humans naturally want to be in control of our own learning, as children and as adults.

I often hear educators refer to research that shows most people need to be engaged to learn. I refute that research; it is not "most people." *All* human beings learn when they are engaged in a real-life struggle with new content (cognitive, affective, or psychomotor content—that is, knowledge, feelings, or skills). In such engagement, learners learn not just the specific content but also the excitement and creative thrill of being decision makers in their own work, of being active learners. When we accept being passive as learners, we are learning how to be passive. What we are doing is what we are learning.

AN EXAMPLE FROM NUTRITION EDUCATION

I spent an hour recently with a nutritionist, who carefully plotted an eating program that would deal with my rising "LDL" (the bad cholesterol) levels. I sat there in some discomfort, knowing how badly I needed to learn this important content. But I was conscious of how little I was learning through this process. While this knowledgeable young man talked and talked, plotting my eating program, explaining why he made this or that choice, I kept saying to myself quietly, over and over, *Me do!*

Imagine another scenario. Imagine what I might learn if I design, from the master sheet, an eating program for myself. Imagine what I might learn as he mentors me, guiding my choices, explaining the rationale behind each of his suggestions. Imagine what might happen if he sets some learning tasks for me.

Imagine if he subscribes to these two assumptions: learners arrive with the capacity to do the work involved in learning, and learners learn when they are actively engaged, cognitively, emotionally, and physically, with the content.

From the way he taught me, I see him holding the opposite of each of these assumptions. The first is that I have not arrived with the capacity to do the work involved in learning. Therefore, I need him to do it for me. He apparently believes I do not need to be actively engaged with the content in order to learn. He assumes I learn by watching him plot a food program and by listening to him.

His assumptions lead to his being engaged in teaching, while I receive his decisions passively. He is not entering into a dialogue but instead presenting a learned monologue, through the food program. It leads to his telling me much that I already know. If he considers our first two assumptions, he will know that I come to this consultation with the capacity to do the work involved in learning and that I will learn this important content if he actively engages and challenges me.

Content and Learning Tasks

The third assumption follows closely on the other two: new content can be presented through learning tasks.

Remember high school science class, where the teacher taught us the unit and then we went to the laboratory to do learning tasks with the materials? That lecture-and-laboratory approach is based on the assumption that new content must first be told and then learned as learners get their hands on it.

Learning tasks integrate lecture and laboratory. A learning task is an excellent way to present new content, inviting engagement and reflection and action on that content. The learning task is not an add-on ("Let's now do a little exercise to see if you've got it"). The learning task is not a testing task. Rather, it is part of an integrated design, presenting new content in a variety of ways, with engaging work for the learner built in. It structures the dialogue.

I must confess to a sinking feeling every time I enter a classroom or conference where a learned teacher is making a "presentation" on a topic. It hurts as I watch adult learners listening, passively, without demanding the opportunity to refute or question what is being taught. Frankly, when I think of how often I did that kind of teaching, in Africa and Asia; in South Harlem and in rural North Carolina; in Bangladesh and in Brooklyn, I blush. As Dan Berrigan, the Jesuit poet-priest, once told us, "When I read my early poetry, a psalm comes to mind: 'Forgive me, O Lord, for the sins of my youth.'"

Just as few teachers would argue the need for engagement, few disagree that content must be designed to fit the learners' context, or that relevance of material is a virtue, or that critical thinking is required to live in a democracy. Few teachers, however, design learning tasks that make their presentation an open question for honest dialogue.

Accountability

This leads to our fourth assumption: learning tasks promote accountability. Teachers are indeed responsible to the learners to design learning tasks that teach the stated content, using appropriate materials. We recognize that learning is an autonomous activity, but it is our job, as adult educators, to produce a design and an environment that invite this learning, that create a learning-centered dialogue.

In respectful dialogue, we examine new cognitive material or psychomotor skills or essential attitudes together, and we engage with this content to learn it anew, to recreate it in ways that make it fit our context.

When I set an appropriate learning task, challenging learners to question and put the new material in context, we all learn, autonomously. The design is accountable.

Using learning tasks can be habit forming. That is, once learners get used to learning by means of learning tasks, they see how they can set such tasks for themselves. They discover that they are learning how to learn. A school project becomes a set of discrete learning tasks sequenced to produce the project and the learning the project manifests. Thesis preparation in a master's program, for instance, becomes a set of learning tasks. Constantly completing learning tasks successfully tells a student something very important about her potential for learning, her accountability to herself.

With only teaching tasks, such as are delineated in curriculum and perhaps in your present lesson plans, there is minimal accountability. You, the teacher, present the material. How do you know they know it? How do they know they know? How has the content been transformed by their engagement with it in their diverse contexts?

A set of learning tasks for a course on American history for adults, taught in Harlem, in rural Arkansas, and in an African American community in Mississippi can invite students to learn that history accountably, by bringing to it their political, economic, and cultural context. As those students do the learning tasks, their diverse contexts shape the history lesson in ways that bring specific significance to it. A traditional presentation cannot do this. At the same time, they are getting the habit of learning.

We can be accountable, through appropriate learning tasks, both to the content and the context, and bring learners to expect to be accountable for their own learning.

Learning Task 2: Reviewing the Four Assumptions

Read again the four assumptions. Describe for yourself what each might mean in your situation.

1. Learners arrive with the capacity to do the work involved in learning.

2. Learners learn when they are actively engaged with the content.

3. New content can be presented through a learning task.

4. Learning tasks promote accountability.

Gravett and Henning describe the process of such dialogue this way: "Based on Bakhtin's theory which implies teacher, learner and knowledge in a dynamic reciprocal unity, dialogic teaching is proposed as transformative exchange, where teachers and learners are involved in a co-learning and co-teaching process, thereby cultivating the development of an authentic community of learners, characterized by sharing and support, along with cognitive challenge. The crux of dialogic teaching is that the teacher as mediator respectfully listens (in a Bakhtinian sense) to how students apprehend and construe phenomena related to academic themes and then guides them through a process of co-inquiry toward a reflective, scientific understanding" (1998).

Learning Task 3: Learning Tasks Defined

Examine this section on defining a learning task. Tell what you would add to the definition.

A learning task is an open question put to learners who have all the resources they need to respond.

An Open Question

We set a learning task to engage learners in the active learning of substantive, new material. We respect their life experience and their unique context and offer the task as an open question, inviting their reflective response. Some learning tasks take place in the mind (cognitive), some in the heart (affective), and some in the muscles (psychomotor).

For example, the nutrition expert might ask me, "In light of the nutrition data and proposed decisions you have just read, which of these decisions do you see will be most difficult for you?" He might ask, "What do you see as a reasonable exchange between starches and proteins for you on any normal workday? What is the practical use to you of the formula 3 grams of fat to every 100 calories?"

Compare the usual closed questions: "Having read the program, tell me what a starch is." "What is a protein?" "What is the comparative value of fat to calories?" "Why is it necessary to cut down on saturated fats?" "What is the difference between HDL and LDL?"

As you know, in a closed question the teacher knows the answers. Closed questions do not make learning tasks. A learning task is an open question put to learners who have all the resources they need to respond. The open question in the learning task is the heart of the matter, inviting critical thinking, demanding reflection, stimulating creativity. For example, to the nutritionist's first open question ("In light of the nutrition data you have just read, which of these decisions do you see will be most difficult for you?") I might respond, "The hardest part of all this is making my eating habits conscious. And yet that may be the best part for me, as a highly intuitive person who needs to develop her sensing function. Perhaps being conscious even of the numbers of grams and calories involved will make me conscious also of the distinct pleasure involved in different tastes and textures."

Do you see what is happening? Because I am not searching for his answer, I am able to explore the meaning of what I have just read in the nutrition program and conclude the implications of that program for my life, in my personal context. Imagine the quality of learning this invites.

I might respond to the second open question ("What do you see as a reasonable exchange between starches and proteins for you on any normal workday?") this way: "You know, I don't think I understand what you mean by exchange. Does that mean any substitution of proteins for starch is useful? Does it give me carte blanche in my choices?"

Notice how this honest response gives the teacher valuable data about my learning so far. Here is another value to the open question: no response is invalidated. Such an attitude excludes fear as a component of the learning task. The "right" answer is what emerges from an honest response for a learner in his context.

Now the teacher can say to the entire class, or to the individual learner: "Let me walk through that section on exchange again. Jane, your confusion is not unusual. This is a very important concept in nutrition, and we want to be sure I make it clear."

To the third open question ("What is the practical use to you of the formula 3 grams of fat to every 100 calories?") I might respond: "Let me try it out on this package of cereal. It says a serving has 280 calories and 9 grams of fat. If the formula works, it would be better for me if it had 3 grams of fat. So this cereal would not be the one I choose."

Do you now see how the open question invites inductive and experience-based reflection, review of the input, reinforcement, and application? In Chapter Four we examine these four aspects in detail.

The Resources They Need to Respond

Every learning task involves a solid, substantive set of resources that the learners use to respond to the open questions. These resources are the new content (ideas, feelings, and skills). They can be presented to the learners in a lecture, an illustrated talk, a video clip, a slide show, a learned article that they all read, a summary article, an outline, a model, a story. . . . The list is virtually infinite. Note that we begin a learning task either inductively (examining the life, history, and context of the learner as they relate to the topic) or deductively (examining the latest content).

For example, the nutritionist can set a learning task asking the class to write everything they eat on a given day—breakfast, lunch, dinner, snacks. This is inductive work. Then, the next learning task asks them to use this data as they examine new content: a model of a low-cholesterol food program. This is deductive work.

Or, the nutritionist may start with the written model, inviting learners to circle on it all the foods they like and want to keep in their program. Then, the learning task asks them to write out all the food they ate yesterday, putting each item into the categories on the model (protein, starches, vegetables, milk products, fats). They can then consider how they want to bring their usual eating patterns into line with the model. This is first deductive work (theory into practice) and then inductive work (practice to theory). Obviously we can use either an inductive-deductive or deductive-inductive approach, depending on the content and the group. Our task as teachers and designers of curriculum is to be conscious of which one we are using, and why.

In Chapter Three we examine how the seven steps of planning clarify exactly what that content is and how appropriate it is for the particular learners. In the nutrition example I offer, it is not useful for the nutritionist to offer me the chemical composition of proteins, starches, and fats, even though he knows it. I do not need to know this in my context, and I cannot learn it accountably in the time we have together.

I started out saying that using learning tasks involves humility. A good teacher does not teach all that he knows. He teaches all that the learners need to know at the time, and all that the learners can accountably learn in the time given.

I see that there is no substantive knowledge (concepts, skills, attitudes) that cannot be taught using learning tasks. Imagine using learning tasks in a history course for adults:

> Having read the chapter on the Civil War, name one of the leaders from both sides whom you would like to interview. Design that interview and the responses you expect him to offer.
>
> Using a map of Virginia, show the areas where the two armies met. Include whatever information you have about each encounter.
>
> Watch one session of Ken Burns's TV program on the Civil War. How does it differ from what you read in our textbook? Offer some reasons for the difference.

One constant response to this challenge to adult educators to design and use learning tasks is "I simply don't have time for this kind of preparation. I can't give that kind of attention to the design of my teaching. It's too expensive in time and money to work this way."

My question is this: What does it cost to teach without ensuring that learning takes place? What is the price of adult learners' failing to grasp essential skills, knowledge, and attitudes? Also, what does it cost to teach without inviting critical thinking and creativity? I work with many graduate students who are struggling to write their dissertations. I propose that they would have a great deal more confidence and ability if they had learned through learning tasks since their preschool days. We honor the fact that it takes courage to use learning tasks, to change one's usual and familiar practice. The noticeable joy of learners in their learning is the best tribute to that courage.

Learning Task 4: Application

Examine the three learning tasks you have already been asked to do in this chapter. Consider how well they apply this definition: "A learning task is an open question put to learners who have all the resources they need to respond."

You will see as you continue through this book that the learning task is not an "exercise." It must be completely integrated into the overall design: teaching the content accountably, achieving the objectives comprehensively, engaging the learners fully. Designing and using learning tasks can change how a teacher defines teaching. Consider at this point how the design of this chapter as a set of learning tasks helps you learn the assumptions behind, and the definition of, learning tasks.

Synthesis

In Chapter One, by completing four short learning tasks you have examined four assumptions about learning tasks, and you have edited a definition of a learning task. You have read Gravett and Henning's description of the process of what they call dialogic teaching. In Chapter Two, we compare and contrast teaching tasks and learning tasks.

2

Comparing Teaching Tasks and Learning Tasks

Learning Task 5

Recently I attended the Lilly Foundation Conference on College Teaching in Towson, Maryland, near Baltimore. I had prepared a ninety-minute session using a series of learning tasks to demonstrate the power of the learning task as an instrument for designing effective teaching. While waiting for my scheduled session, I attended a number of others where college professors presented approaches to successful, engaging college teaching.

Doing What We Teach

This analysis looks at the *where* (site) and *who* (roles of professor and learners), and the materials used in teaching.

The Site

The rooms, in a hotel conference center, were set up for presentations: overhead projectors, slide projectors, large screens at the front, a lectern for the presenter, and individual writing desk chairs for participants.

I asked instead for a new configuration of the room for my session: tables with six chairs at each, because I wanted participants to do the designed learning tasks in small groups.

Roles

In the presentations I attended, the leader spoke and the learners listened. The leaders put the outline and accompanying illustrations of their talk on the large screen, and we looked at these as we listened.

There was no structuring of our engagement beyond listening and looking, and at the end of the presentation we heard the leader's inevitable inquiry: "Are there any questions?"

We participants never had occasion in these sessions to meet one another; nor did we exchange our impressions of the presentation. We left with handouts of the material that had been on the large screen. We never got to struggle with the content being presented, or to do anything that involved active learning.

It is likely that all of these professors agree with the learning theory proposing that learners must construct their own learning through active engagement with new concepts, skills, and attitudes. But we did not see it applied in sessions that used teaching tasks.

In the session using learning tasks, by contrast, men and women at their tables of six got to tell their own stories as they introduced themselves to one another. They critically examined the content and achievement-based objectives of the session and identified their expectations. They worked hard, doing six learning tasks, sharing creative conclusions and questions. At the end of the ninety minutes, they knew that they knew what we had proposed they learn through the design. They also had met one another and struggled with the content together, as peers and partners, constructing their knowledge.

My role puzzled many of them. I offered an initial introduction to the process, then set the tasks, led the sharing of conclusions and questions, kept time, and brought the session to a close by inviting them to reflect on how many of their expectations had been met. They were frankly puzzled by how little I did during the session. It was indeed a new role for the professor.

Materials

In the other presentations I attended, professors used Microsoft PowerPoint charts projected on the overhead to accompany the lecture. Often a summary of these overheads was offered as a handout.

In the session using learning tasks, participants received the session design, which you can find in Appendix A. This program included the content, achievement-based objectives, and learning tasks. They could follow the program using this material, and take it home as a mnemonic, reminding them how to use the seven steps and how to design learning tasks.

One of the professors in my session, an historian from Belmont University in Tennessee, said, "I noticed that you did what you were teaching."

Learning Task 5: Differences Between Teaching Tasks and Learning Tasks

Here are two examples of courses for adults.

Task 5A

Read over these two presentations.

PRESENTATION ONE (WITH TEACHING TASKS): A ONE-HOUR MUSIC CLASS IN AN ELDERHOSTEL COURSE

TITLE: THE LIFE AND WORK OF VERDI

The professor opens his presentation by using a slide show with pictures of composer Giuseppe Verdi's life, showing him and his family and associates, and sites in Italy and France where he lived and worked. The professor accompanies the slide show with a lecture, describing each person and site. The slide show, which is accompanied by musical pieces where appropriate, is based on the life of Verdi by Mary Jane

Phillips-Matz (1993). At the end of this slide show, the professor asks one closed question: "Are there any questions?"

This professor is knowledgeable and lively in his explanations of all of the pictures in the slide show. He shares a great deal of information about Verdi through the slide show and his comments. There are no questions from the learners in response to his final query.

PRESENTATION TWO (DIALOGUE—A DESIGN WITH LEARNING TASKS): A ONE-HOUR CLASS IN AN ELDERHOSTEL COURSE

TITLE: THE LIFE AND WORK OF VERDI

VERDI LEARNING TASK 1: WHO, WHERE, AND WHEN Each table has a large map of Europe with certain locations marked, a picture of Verdi, and a list of his operas along with the sites of their premiere performances.

Task 1A: examine this map of Europe. Note the photograph of Verdi as a man of eighty. Look over the sites related to his life: his birthplace in Italy; his pastoral home in Sant'Agata; and Paris, London, Milan (La Scala), Venice (La Fenice), and Rome. Remember that the time is 1814 to 1901. This was before the jet airplane, and even before the gasoline engine. Examine the list of Verdi's operas and the places where they were first performed.

Task 1B: share with your table group one thing this geography lesson tells you about this artist. We'll hear a sampling of comments.

VERDI LEARNING TASK 2: VIVA VERDI Task 2A: watch this slide show, and read this short summary description of the facts in the slide show.

Verdi was born in 1814 and died in 1901, so his life spanned much of the nineteenth century. He came from Bussetto, a town in rural Italy. As a youth, he was not accepted at the prestigious music school to which he applied because the professors said he did not show enough skill and knowledge.

Verdi's first wife died in the third year of their marriage, shortly after the death of their two infant daughters. His operas feature the theme of family, especially the relation of daughters and fathers (as examples, *Simon Boccanegra* and *Rigoletto*).

Verdi was a staunch patriot and was once actually elected a member of the Chamber of Deputies. "Viva Vittore Emmanuele Re d'Italia" is what patriots at the time wrote on walls, hidden as an acronym: VIVA VERDI.

Circle one item in this brief description that speaks to you. Share at your table what you circled and why. We'll hear a sampling of answers.

VERDI LEARNING TASK 3: THE MUSIC Listen to these two arias from two of Verdi's operas, *La Traviata* and *Aïda*. Read the words of the arias on the handout.

Describe at your table what you hear in this music of the themes from Verdi's life that you examined in learning tasks 1 and 2.

Task 5B

Name at least two differences you perceived between the two presentations.

The traditional presentation assumes that the learners are willing to be passive. It presumes that they bring little to the learning event. This presentation also supposes that learning takes place by imparting information. It is based on a theory of knowledge that sees it as shared data. It does not engage the learner at the level of critical thought and critical feeling.

Lectures and Learning Tasks

Lectures are integral to learning tasks as one way of offering new input. New research or information must be presented cogently and clearly, as part of a learning task. The lecture is input, which, as we have mentioned and shall see again later, is one of the four elements that make up an effective learning session (inductive work, input, implementation, integration).

However, learning is more than gathering new information. Bloom's *Taxonomy of Educational Objectives* says, "There is little doubt that our culture places tremendous weight on knowledge or information as an important characteristic of the individual. . . . Because of the simplicity of teaching and evaluating knowledge, it [information] is frequently emphasized as an educational objective out of all proportion to its usefulness or its relevance for the development of the individual" (1956, p. 34).

In the first example, learners got significant information about Giuseppe Verdi and his life by means of the slide show and the professor's explanations. In the session using learning tasks, learners were invited to use their creativity and to make a synthesis. The same information was shared; the same slide show was used. However, the information was used as a set of materials to catalyze analysis and synthesis, creative work and argument. Learners were engaged, in small groups and in the large group, in constructing, not just in receiving, content.

Learning tasks engage learners in a dialogue about the content: the dates of Verdi's life, significant themes in his operas, meaningful sites in his life, and a sample of his music.

Here is another example, again showing a presentation using teaching tasks and a design using learning tasks.

Task 5C

Identify the differences you perceive between these two sessions on a technology topic.

PRESENTATION ONE (DESIGN USING TEACHING TASKS)

TITLE: USING THE INTERNET FOR ELECTRONIC MAIL

In an uninterrupted lecture, the presenter talks about the history of the Internet, who designed it, how it was implemented, and how it has grown. He indicates that e-mail is one of the most popular uses of this resource. He tells the learners the names of five or six common e-mail suppliers or connectors to the Internet (AOL, MSN, etc.). He offers them free CD-ROMs from each of these suppliers to start an Internet account. Then he gives a demonstration, using an overhead projection from his computer, in which he opens his own electronic mailbox, reads a piece of mail, and closes it. Then he asks, "Are there any questions?"

(If this example sounds exaggerated, let me tell you that I experienced a community college teacher do exactly that at a class I paid for and attended very recently. We spent the first three of five sessions listening to the professor, never touching a computer.)

PRESENTATION TWO (DESIGN USING LEARNING TASKS)

TITLE: OPENING AN E-MAIL ACCOUNT AND USING IT

Here are the achievement-based objectives:

In completing this six-hour session, all participants, all of whom have access to a computer, will have:

- Examined the process of opening and using e-mail
- Examined the offerings of several providers (AOL, Mindspring, etc.)
- Decided on one provider
- Set up an e-mail account

- Practiced sending and receiving e-mail
- Practiced downloading a file

E-MAIL LEARNING TASK 1: THE PROCESS OF OPENING AND USING E-MAIL Watch this demonstration as I open my e-mail, read a note, and download a file to send with my reply. What are your questions?

E-MAIL LEARNING TASK 2A: DIFFERENCES BETWEEN PROVIDERS Insert the CD from AOL. Set up a temporary account by following the directions given. What strikes you about the main page?

E-MAIL LEARNING TASK 2B: SENDING AN E-MAIL Send an e-mail to me at my address. Let me reply. Read your mail. Walk through the services of AOL. What are your questions?

E-MAIL LEARNING TASK 2C: COMPARING ANOTHER PROVIDER Now use the Mindspring CD. Set up a temporary account by following the directions given. What strikes you about their main page?

E-MAIL LEARNING TASK 2D: SENDING AN E-MAIL WITH ANOTHER PROVIDER Send an e-mail to me at my address. Let me reply. Read your mail. Walk through the services of Mindspring. What are your questions?

E-MAIL LEARNING TASK 3A: SET UP AN ACCOUNT Make a decision and set up your own temporary account using one of the providers. Follow the setup steps. What are your questions?

E-MAIL LEARNING TASK 3B: SENDING AN E-MAIL WITH NEWLY ESTABLISHED ACCOUNT Download a file to send with an e-mail. Send me your e-mail at my address. Delete, or file, the e-mail you sent me. What are your questions?

Notice how these tasks are carefully sequenced. Through guided practice the tasks build skills that are incremental, one leading to the next. Note also that there is virtually no need for a prolonged lecture; this learning occurs by reflection on the actions. It takes place through their questions. In this case it is almost entirely inductive, that is, moving from action to theory.

What other distinctions do you observe between the two processes? Can you see why we say that a learning task is an open question put to learners who have the resources they need to respond? The directives (set up, make a file, delete the file), followed by "What are your questions?" are in fact all open questions. Can you see why we say that a learning task is addressed to learners seen as decision makers in their own learning?

How many opportunities for decision making do you see in the Verdi and e-mail learning tasks? We can only let adults know we perceive them as subjects or decision makers in their own learning by treating them as such.

Learning, Transfer, Impact

In our book on evaluation, *How Do They Know They Know* (Vella, Berardinelli, and Burrow, 1998), we mentioned three aspects of an educational session that must be evaluated: (1) learning that occurs during a session, (2) transfer (use of new skills, knowledge, and attitudes in a workplace setting), and (3) impact (the change in the organization's approach brought about by the learning and transfer). The accountability of teaching can be measured by examining all three: learning, transfer, and impact. Consider the potential of learning, transfer, and impact after a presentation with only teaching tasks, and after a session using learning tasks.

Synthesis

In Chapter Two, we have seen in the opening story an event from a conference where the difference between teaching tasks and learning tasks is clear. We have examined two further examples, one from an adult music history course and the other from a course on technology skills. In Chapter Three, we see how an entire course can be designed with learning tasks that implement objectives and teach content, and in Chapter Four we look more closely at the four types of learning task: inductive, input, implementation, and integration.

3

Learning Tasks As Part of a Complete Design

Learning Task 6

Meals on Wheels and the Inter-Faith Food Shuttle in Wake County, North Carolina, are two quiet, powerful not-for-profit groups that are leading a revolution. Each in its own way strives to ensure that no one in this county goes to bed hungry. They recently decided to build a facility with offices and a large kitchen in common. In this community kitchen, foods saved from county restaurants can be shaped into delicious, deliverable units to serve the hungry.

Imagine getting the boards of directors of two vital organizations to agree on such a risky project. To facilitate their decision, we decided to do a strategic-planning program for the group that was designing the capital campaign and the integrated project. As I presented the seven steps of planning to the committee and we worked through them to design appropriate learning tasks, one member exclaimed, "This is a very useful tool!"

The Seven Steps of Planning

1. *Who*: participants, leaders, the number of participants

2. *Why*: the situation that calls for this educational program

3. *When*: the time frame

4. *Where*: the site

5. *What*: the content: skills, knowledge, attitudes
6. *What for*: achievement-based objectives
7. *How*: learning tasks and materials

We designed six learning tasks for the teams from Meals on Wheels and the Inter-Faith Food Shuttle. Then, as we worked through the program, we found ourselves stopped at the fourth learning task. The dialogue and learning going on during that task were so intense that it was easy to decide not to go further. We never completed the final two learning tasks because we did not need them. Our plan was sound enough to allow us to abandon it. The seven steps proved a useful tool, indeed.

In the following example of a session teaching another group the strategic-planning process, we shall see how the learning task, the *how* of the seven steps, is connected to the *what* (content) and the *what for* (achievement-based objectives).

Learning Task 6: The Connection: Content, Objectives, Tasks

Here is a design for a six-hour session, teaching a model for strategic planning. It is based on John Bryson's popular *Strategic Planning for Public and Nonprofit Organizations* (1988).

Task 6A

Read this design, which uses the seven steps of planning. Note anywhere you see the connection between learning tasks (*how*) and the other six steps: *who, why, when, where, what*, and *what for*.

Who (Participants). Thirty not-for-profit directors and program coordinators representing fifteen nonprofit organizations in Durham, North Carolina.

Why (The Situation). These directors and program coordinators need to design a strategic plan for their respective organizations to work well. They need to have a clear model for such strategic planning since all funding agencies demand such a plan. They will take this model home and use it with their staff and board.

When (the Time Frame). A one-day course, six hours.

Where (the Site). A room at the community center: five tables with six people at a table; flipcharts and felt pens, an overhead projector.

What (the Content). The meaning of strategic planning; mission statement; stakeholders; a SWOT analysis (internal: strengths, weaknesses; external: opportunities, threats); strategic issues; strategies; action steps on a time line.

What for (Achievement-Based Objectives). By the end of this six-hour course, all participants will have:

1. Identified the stakeholders of their not-for-profit agency. Stakeholders are all those who have a stake in the mission of the agency.
2. Defined and practiced designing a mission statement. The mission is the reason why the organization exists.
3. Begun a SWOT analysis of their agency at present.
4. Identified one strategic issue facing their organization. Strategic issues are those that affect the entire operation.
5. Named one strategy to address the issue identified in objective four.
6. Described their vision of this strategy in place (alternatives, dreams, visions of a new reality).

7. Identified at least one action that brings about this vision and puts this action on a time line.

How: Learning Tasks and Materials

Here are the learning tasks designed to teach strategic planning.

STRATEGIC-PLANNING LEARNING TASK 1:
WARM-UP—GOOD PLANNING

Task 1A: In pairs, with someone from another agency, talk about one time in your life when you made a plan and implemented it. Tell the other person why you think it worked for you. Write each reason on a Post-it note. Put them on Chart 1, "Our Reasons for Success in Planning." We'll hear all the reasons.

Task 1B: At your table, talk about how your reasons for success are congruent with this definition of a strategic plan:

A strategic plan is designed to guide an organization in its choice of actions by making everyone conscious of mission, stakeholders' needs and hope, an analysis of the resources of the organization, and internal and external issues. It names desired actions and steps to implement those actions.

We'll hear a sample of your responses.

STRATEGIC-PLANNING LEARNING TASK 2:
PROGRAM REVIEW AND EXPECTATIONS

Task 2A: Listen to the achievement-based objectives and content of this short course. Look at the seven learning tasks. What are your questions?

Task 2B: In new pairs, name your personal expectations of this course. Write each on a card, initial it, and post it. We'll hear all, and we'll refer to them at the end of our session.

STRATEGIC-PLANNING LEARNING TASK 3: STAKEHOLDER ANALYSIS

A stakeholder is someone who has a stake in the success of the organization.

Task 3A: In agency pairs, name the stakeholders of your organization. That is, who has a stake in the success of your work? Complete the agency chart of stakeholders.

Task 3B: Share your chart of stakeholders at your table with people from two other agencies. Examine theirs.

Task 3C: What are your questions about stakeholder analysis?

STRATEGIC-PLANNING LEARNING TASK 4: MISSION OF YOUR AGENCY

The mission is the reason the agency exists and what it hopes to do.

Task 4A: In your agency pair, review the given mission of your organization, or prepare one using the model offered.

Task 4B: Share your mission statement with the others at your table, and examine theirs.

Task 4C: What are your questions?

STRATEGIC-PLANNING LEARNING TASK 5: A SWOT ANALYSIS

Task 5A: In your agency pair, begin a SWOT analysis of your not-for-profit. Name one item under each category.

- Internal: strengths
- Internal: weaknesses
- External: opportunities
- External: threats

Task 5B: Share your beginning SWOT analysis with others at your table.

Task 5C: What are your questions? We'll hear them all.

STRATEGIC-PLANNING LEARNING TASK 6: ISSUES AND STRATEGY

Task 6A: In your agency pair, name one problem or issue you face.

A strategic issue is an issue or problem that affects all operations. For example, in our organization a strategic issue is quality control of courses since we contract with associates.

Task 6B: Describe a strategy or guideline for action that deals with this strategic issue.

Task 6C: Share your strategic issue and strategy for this issue with the others at your table.

STRATEGIC-PLANNING LEARNING TASK 7: VISION OF THE STRATEGY IN PLACE

Task 7A: In your agency pair, describe what the strategy would look like in place at your agency.

For example, in our organization the job description of the program coordinator includes reviewing videotapes of all courses. A video camera is already in place for all courses, so we need to be sure there is a blank tape marked for the course. Payment to contract associates accompanies a written review of the videotaped portion of the course. This ensures quality control of all teaching.

Task 7B: Share your vision of the strategy that is in place with others at your table. Listen to theirs.

STRATEGIC-PLANNING LEARNING TASK 8: ACTIONS NEEDED

In our example, four actions are called for:

1. Revise the job description of the program coordinator.
2. Prepare a protocol for all contract associates that will be included in their contract.

3. Add a marked blank videotape to the list of course materials.

4. Prepare a matrix for feedback on the reviewed video.

   Task 8A: In your agency pair, set out the actions needed to implement the strategy. Put the actions in a reasonable sequence on the "Force Field" chart, considering what actions move the strategy, who carries them out, by when, and when they are checked for completion.

   Our example is in Table 3.1.

Task 8B: Share your sequence of actions with others at your table.

Task 8C: What are your questions?

STRATEGIC-PLANNING LEARNING TASK 9: SYNTHESIS AND REVIEW

Task 9A: Examine at your table what you all have produced as a draft strategic plan. Tell the others what surprises you about what your agency did or what others have done.

   Task 9B: Identify, by name and office, who in your agency or on your board you would like to see learn this process. We'll hear a sampling of answers.

   Task 9C: Review the section headings in Bryson's *Strategic Planning for Public and Nonprofit Organizations*. What are your questions about these concepts and practices?

TABLE 3.1 Sample of Strategic Actions.

Actions	Who	By When	Check
Revise the job description	Program coordinator	3/28	
Write protocol	Director	2/28	
Prepare videotape	Program coordinator	2/28	
Prepare matrix	Program staff	2/28	

Task 9D: Review what you wrote for your expectations of this course in learning task 1, and review the seven achievement-based objectives. What strikes you about this material?

What did you observe as connections between the content, objectives, and learning tasks? The *who* (participants) component controls everything. It controls what time frame is useful for this group, what objectives will work, what learning tasks are designed. Learning tasks have to be appropriate to a particular group of people. We could not, for example, ask this strategic-planning group to go into detail on setting up financial systems for their agencies, since they are not the finance officers. We would not design a learning task that speaks in the abstract about the philosophy of their organizations because these are action folks who want to get their agencies into gear. Fitting the *how* to the *who*, the learning tasks to the participants, is vital in designing effective programs.

The time frame (*when*) is another operative question. It is easy to prepare too much *what* and *how* for the *when*, that is, to deal with too much content and design too many learning tasks for the time allotted. Notice in the example above that we have nine learning tasks for a six-hour framework. You can take that as a rule of thumb: at least one learning task for each piece of content, and one or two to set the stage and complete the session. With thirty people, a forty-minute average time frame for a learning task could work in this case. In Chapter Eight, we look closely at this issue of timing.

In most sessions, we take a break after each learning task. This physical change is important for learners and leaders. Remember: the danger is to design too much *what* for the *when*. Our challenge is to design not only effective learning tasks to teach the content but also an effective overall program, with an eye on the available time frame.

Now, let's examine the relationship you noted between the learning tasks and the content (*what*) and the achievement-based objectives (*what for*). Essentially, the objectives are what the learners do to learn the content: the *what for* implements the *what*. I trust you noticed that an efficient, succinct, well-written, achievement-based objective has the learning task already in it.

Here is an example of the connection between *what, what for,* and *how*:

- *What*: content (strategic issues of participants)
- *What for*: achievement-based objective (identify one strategic issue facing their organization)
- *How*: strategic-planning learning task 6 (strategic issues; "In your agency pair, name one strategic issue you face. A strategic issue is an issue or problem that affects all operations.")

As you design using this seven-step template, you will see the direct correlation between the content, the objectives, and the learning tasks. The inner harmony in these designs creates safety for the learner, who soon sees the correlation and recognizes how the design is accountable, clearly teaching the named content.

Notice how the verbs in the achievement-based objectives often become the verbs in the learning tasks. When you design an appropriate achievement-based objective (*what for*) to teach the content (*what*) for this particular group (*who*) in this unique situation (*why*), you actually design a major part of the learning tasks (*how*). Later, in Chapter Five, we examine verbs that work well in learning tasks.

You will see when you begin to use learning tasks how this correlation works: changing the learning task changes the achievement-based objective, which can change the content. These two, task and objective, are in what the philosopher Hegel calls "a dialectical relationship."

Synthesis

In Chapter Three, by doing one learning task we have reviewed the seven steps of planning as a useful tool in designing effective adult learning. We have shown the relationship between the participants (*who*), situation (*why*), time frame (*when*), site (*where*), content (*what*), and objectives (*what for*) and the learning tasks and materials (*how*). In Chapter Four, we examine the four types of learning tasks: inductive, input, implementation, and integration.

4

Four Types of Learning Tasks

Learning Tasks 7 and 8

In 1994, as a group of adult educators struggled in an adult education workshop with the concept and skill of designing learning tasks, my colleague Fernando Menendez and I struggled ourselves to design a model they could use to enlighten and lighten their task. We both realized they needed some instrument or tool to guide them.

We decided that any effective design needs four components: (1) a learning task that connects learners with what they already know and with their unique context; (2) a learning task that invites them to examine new input (concepts, skills, or attitudes)—the content of the course; (3) a learning task that gets learners to do something directly with that new content, somehow implementing it; and finally, (4) a learning task that integrates this new learning into their lives. Menendez and I called this model the four I's:

1. Inductive work
2. Input
3. Implementation
4. Integration

Although the teams in the workshop on adult education struggled to design learning tasks, we decided to introduce the model *after* the first practice design and team teaching. We did this for two reasons. First, the group had so much new information as they began the first design that this model would be lost. Also, it would mean a great deal to all of them to see that they incorporated it in-tuitively into their first design. The model became a corroboration of their good intuition.

It was a delightful experience to watch the teams recognize that they had in fact already been using this model they were apparently just learning. Virtually all of their designs, in some way or another, naturally used this sequence of learning tasks: some inductive work, input, implementation of the new content, and integration.

They all laughed when they saw the model applied so naturally to their initial designs. One person said aloud what we were all thinking: "We're learning what we already knew!"

Learning Task 7: A Model for Planning a Session (Four I's)

Task 7A: Select a recent teaching that you have done. Sketch it into learning tasks instead of teaching tasks. Set out four learning tasks, in this order: (1) inductive work (related to life), (2) input (new content), (3) implementation (doing something with input), and (4) integration (moving new learning into life). Before you do your own design, follow the example in the next section.

How Do They Know They Know?

I recently designed and taught a short course on the basic elements in our evaluation book, *How Do They Know They Know*. I started with the seven steps of planning:

1. *Who*: A small group of educators and administrators from a community college.

2. *Why*: They are dissatisfied with their present assessment and evaluation system. They agreed to give one day, five hours, to examine the basics in our approach to evaluation. They need to teach all of their instructors how to use these concepts and skills.

3. *When*: Five hours (9:00 A.M. to 12:00 noon and 1:00 to 3:00).

4. *Where*: In a comfortable room at the community college. Five tables with four seated at a table. An easel and flipchart, an overhead projector, and a VCR or monitor.

5. *What* (the content): Learning, transfer, impact; theory of impact; seven steps of evaluation; quantitative and qualitative methods.

6. *What for* (achievement-based objectives): When they have finished the five-hour session, all participants will have

   Distinguished among learning, transfer, and impact

   Used the theory of impact to examine one course of study

   Practiced working with the seven steps of evaluation

   Used both quantitative and qualitative methods

   Examined a case study using the accountability planner

7. *How*: Learning tasks and materials.

Here is where the four I's helped me. I knew I had to do some inductive work prior to teaching each of the new concepts. I wanted to make sure the input was comprehensive and well sequenced. I needed to offer them enough implementation tasks so they would grasp the concepts and feel comfortable with the skills. The workshop was set up so that integration tasks would be done in the two weeks following the workshop, and they would be reviewed as soon as they were completed.

Here is one set of learning tasks for the first content item.

EVALUATION TASK 1: LEARNING, TRANSFER, AND IMPACT

Task 1A (inductive): State one thing you learned that you now use daily in your work or in your life. Tell where you learned that concept or skill. Your use of the skill is transfer.

Task 1B (input): Read this description of learning, transfer, and impact. Circle what is most useful to you.

LEARNING, TRANSFER, AND IMPACT

Learning is what occurs within a program. It is completion of the achievement-based objectives, visible in products and projects. Transfer is using this learning: concepts, skills, and attitudes in another setting, at work or at home. Impact is the measurable change in the organization as a result of the learning and transfer.

Learning, transfer, and impact are three evaluation levels explored in this course. Each is an independent level of evaluation that reveals distinct information. Although separate, these levels of evaluation are also interdependent; that is, without learning, there is no transfer, and without transfer there is no impact.

Learning evaluation involves assessing the degree to which the learner gains new knowledge, skills, or attitudes (KSAs) that result from a program.

Transfer evaluation measures how participants apply their learning to their work and or daily life.

Impact evaluation measures the broad, long-term effect of the project or program on an organization or an individual.

Task 1C (implementation): In pairs, review the concept or skill you described in task 1A. Describe the distinction you now see among learning, transfer, and impact in relation to that knowledge or skill.

Task 1D (integration): At your table, talk about how this distinction among learning, transfer, and impact can help you in your work in this department of the community college. We'll hear a sample of responses.

In this case, the four parts of the learning task fell neatly into the model. Often, the topic calls for a number of tasks. No matter how you organize the learning tasks, the four I's pattern can be a guide toward accountability.

Exhibit 4.1 is a list showing the four types of learning tasks as they were laid out in sequence.

There is clearly a pattern here, a gentle sequence guaranteed to make learning happen for the group. Once they work through all four I's, they can say that they know they know because they just did it, again and again, and received feedback and course correction each time.

EXHIBIT 4.1 The Four I's.

Inductive Work (Learning Task 1A)
Name one thing you have learned that you use daily in your work or in your life. Tell where you learned that concept or skill. Your use of that skill is an example of transfer.

Input (Learning Task 1B)
Read the following description [not included in Exhibit 4.1] of learning, transfer, and impact. Circle what strikes you as vital here. We'll hear all that you circled.

Implementation (Learning Task 1C)
In pairs, review the concept or skill described in learning task 1A. Describe the distinctions you now see among learning, transfer, and impact in relation to that knowledge or skill.

Integration (Learning Task 1D)
At your table, name ways in which these distinctions among learning, transfer, and impact can help you in your work in this department of the community college. We'll hear a sample of your responses.

Let us now examine these four types of learning task, by defining each one, giving an example, and considering together the ongoing research agenda: What other types of learning task do we need to design in order to teach for accountable learning?

Learning Task 8: Four Types of Learning Task in Detail

This learning task demonstrates what the four types can do.

Task 8A

Examine these four definitions and examples. Circle what strikes you as significant.

Inductive Tasks

Some learning tasks do not offer startling new insights or information; instead, they invite learners to clarify where they are, at present, in terms of new content; where they begin their study; and what their present conception of the topic includes. Inductive tasks can use the verbs *describe, tell the story of, define, sketch, show, name,* etc. Look at the implied open question in learning task 1 above: Name one thing you have learned that you now use daily in your work or in your life.

This is an inductive task. It is inductive in that it begins with the lives and experiences of the learners. It is an open question, assuming their capacity to say, as subjects or decision makers of their own learning, just what learning means to them. It involves using an open question demanding priority—the best learning experience.

Comparison is an instrument widely used in learning tasks. For example, to open a history class on the U.S. Civil War, two inductive tasks using comparison might be:

1. How would the questions you might ask a Confederate Army soldier differ from those you would ask a Union Army soldier?

2. Here are the two flags: for the Union and the flag of the Confederacy. What differences do you see in their symbolism?

An inductive learning task I use when leading orientation courses for new members in an industry is this: How does your experience in being hired by this company differ from your experience in other companies for which you have worked?

What does an inductive task do? It sets the stage for learning by sharpening the perception of the learner. It tells the learner not only what he or she has to learn but also what the person perceives he or she knows already. Sometimes this is a rude awakening, sometimes a corroborating experience. The shared results of such reflection offer information about learners to a discerning teacher, as well as information about the discerning teacher to the learners. The dialogue begins.

Here are four further examples of inductive learning tasks:

1. (Physics) Describe your first physics class. Talk about what most surprised you.

2. (Chemistry) This is our textbook. Examine the table of contents. Name the chapter or section that most excites you. Name the one that most intimidates you just by its title.

3. (Social geography) Name your favorite places in the world: those you have seen and lived in, those you have been to in literature or through films, and those you have visited on the Internet. What beguiles you about each place? Choose one of those places and describe the question you want to put to an old woman who lives there today.

4. (Computers 101) Describe your first use of a computer. Talk about what was most surprising and what was most intimidating. Name one absolutely essential use of the computer that you anticipate will be invented soon.

Sometimes, an inductive learning task can be used as a warm-up in a program. Remember that a warm-up is always a learning task; it is never a peripheral or slight "exercise." What is substantive about an inductive task? Here is where our epistemology comes into play. If we recognize that all knowing is incremental, and new KSAs are based on what has gone before, we honor the experience and perception of learners. Their prior knowledge is sacred content, idiosyncratic, unique, and utterly determined by sociopolitical and economic context. We honor it as true knowing, not as the end but as the beginning of new knowing.

In most inductive tasks, the content of a learner's perception is the substance of the task. How quickly learners discern if a teacher disdains or respects the true content! We need to design ways to measure our own level of respect for learners.

In *Leadership and the New Science* (1999), Margaret Wheatley describes significant experiments showing how all matter is connected. Carl Jung told us that "the psyche knows no time." So our inductive work aims to connect new knowing with old, and prior knowledge with new content.

When learners do a well-designed inductive task, they are connecting to their lifelong experience of the new content they are learning. They can then self-motivate to the struggle that is involved in learning the new content.

The word *motivation* comes from the Latin word for moving. In the physics of education, we know that one person cannot move another; one only moves oneself. In our effort toward accountable learning-centered education, we know that the only motivation that is not dominating is self-motivation. Imagine the self-motivation of learners who have clarified not only what the new learning is about but also what they perceive it can do to enhance their lives.

Input Tasks

Input tasks invite the learner to grapple directly with new content. In an input task the new content (KSA) is presented, the challenge is set, and the gauntlet is thrown: do something with this in order to learn it. Input tasks involve presenting substantive concepts, data, skill sets, and attitudes for examination, comparison, reflection, practice, editing, rearranging, and reconstructing. In Chapter Five, we examine the verbs that make input tasks come to life.

Presenting new content is done within the framework of a learning task. Consider a project-management learning task, which teaches twelve project-management steps. In this learning task, the learners work through the twelve steps in terms of their context. (I have replaced the number of the learning task and its subtasks with "#" to avoid confusing this material with the other learning tasks in this chapter.)

AN INPUT TASK (LEARNING TASK #: A NEW APPROACH TO PROJECT MANAGEMENT)

Task #A: Examine the twelve cards you have on your table; they give you the steps of this new approach to project management. Put them in a reasonable sequence for your projects. When you have completed the sequence at your table, look at what people at other tables have done with the same steps.

Task #B: Listen to the sequence we used in a recent project for developing new software. Look at this sequence on the overhead projections.

Task #C: At your table, compare what you suggested would be a useful sequence and how we used the twelve steps. Identify the differences. We'll hear a sample of your observations.

Task #D: At your table, name other steps that you all think it would be useful to include. Name any steps in the sequence you see as unnecessary. Write them on Post-it cards and put them up on a chart.

Input tasks differ from inductive tasks in that the new material is met head on. The design challenge is not to present this new material as static fact but as an integral part of a learning task, for learners to work over, struggle with, contest, and actually recreate to fit their context.

We have reached the heart of the matter. In *Education, Modernity, and Fractured Meaning* (1989), Donald Oliver speaks of the need for what he calls "constructed knowing." He describes this as the result of a learner struggling with knowledge until it is her own, until the concepts, skills, or attitudes learned begin to look like her, feel like her, take her shape. In a sense, the epistemology of dialogue invites us to recreate what we learn so that it fits our world.

Oliver compares such knowing to what he labels "received knowing," where the KSAs are accepted passively and repeated in the life of the learner. In the approach to adult learning offered in this book, such passivity is reprehensible. Received knowing is what occurs when learners are passive. It is not what we consider worthy fruit of education.

In *Teaching in Practice* (1995), Andy Farquharson shows the difference between positivist inquiry and constructivism. In positivist inquiry, he says, "The locus of control is primarily the teacher. Teaching is tightly structured and learning outcomes are stated in behavioral terms" (p. 28). Constructivism proposes that each of us creates or constructs the reality we experience, and so we must recreate the theory that explains the reality.

Gravett and Henning describe this phenomenon in this way:

> Dialogue as transformative exchange is based on more than knowledge as purely a matter of cognition. Many authors emphasize the affective pillars of safety, connectedness and respect as well as a realistic hopeful view of people and their capacity to change (Caine and Caine, 1991, Vella, 1994, Shor, 1992, Wlodkowski and Ginsberg, 1996). Learning, from a dialogic perspective, is thus viewed as social construction of personal knowledge, involving a conjunction of the rational and the emotional. "Dialogic" teachers are concerned with the "constant dialectic interplay" between ". . . how learners construe (or interpret) events and ideas and how they construct (build or assemble) structures of meaning" (Candy, 1991, p. 272). The dialogic teaching perspective we have adopted aims at guiding learners to construct deep under-

standing; [to] develop the thought characteristics typical of a skilled practitioner in the field of study; and to act from reflection, instead of memorizing and repeating facts and theories "transferred" to them or, worse, "downloaded" onto them.

The dialogic pillars of respect and safety imply "that the integrity of each person is valued in ways that welcome the worth and expression of one's true self without fear of threat or blame. In such an atmosphere, people know they are respected because they feel safe, capable, and accepted" (Wlodkowski and Ginsberg, 1996, p. 62). Connectedness entails an awareness that one is cared for and one cares for others in the learning group. The pillar of a realistic hopeful view of people and their capacity to change should not be confused with a "superficial mentality of clichés on buttons and bumper stickers" (Wlodkowski and Ginsberg, 1996, p. 70). We believe students are capable of meaningful learning when their current views are respected and they are assured of the appropriate degree of safety and opportunity to explore. Caine and Caine (1991, p. 134) maintain that students can overcome some of their immediate limitations when they are in a state of "relaxed alertness," relaxed alertness being a state of mind when students experience low threat and a pervasive sense of wellbeing in combination with moderate to high challenge. A dialogic approach to teaching and learning can be highlighted by contrasting it with a monologic approach with regard to knowledge, learners, the teacher, relationships and context.

What we offer in this book is a structured approach to that dialogue, which respects the cultural context of the learners. Consider how this relates to the research done by Mary Belenky and her colleagues in *Women's Ways of Knowing* (1986). When they interviewed hundreds of women, they discovered a developmental process in which a woman moved from accepting the knowledge offered by an esteemed teacher, to questioning it as it fit her life, to shaping the knowledge so that it had meaning and use in her context.

This is scientific method, praxis at its best. When I present a theory, model, data, or an interpretation of history using an input task, I invite learners to examine it, question it, refute it if they have the means, and make it theirs through a real struggle.

This is not to denigrate in any way present research or the solidity of data and facts in the textbooks. We know, however, that those textbooks are outdated before the ink is dry because of exciting developments in research and the growth of knowledge. Learners can learn how to learn by working on input tasks that challenge them and respect their culture and context.

The epistemology of dialogue on which we build the argument for learning tasks maintains that *knowing* is an active verb, and that all valid knowing is idiosyncratic, personal, and culturally specific.

When I learn to fly an airplane, I learn the same set of concepts, skills, and attitudes as my fellow pilots. I always stamp these with my own specific and peculiar fingerprint. No two dancers in the Carolina Ballet Company express themselves in quite the same way, yet their harmonic movement is exquisite. Because it is human, it is not mechanical, but at once structured and idiosyncratic.

Constructed knowing, as Oliver defines it, is the only knowing that holds up under moral or political or economic pressure. An input learning task sets up a dynamic reciprocal unity, holding the opposites as Jung advises, between the accrued knowledge of the professor and the person, culture, and context of the learner. Jung offered a vital secret in terms of motivation: holding the opposites creates tension that accesses energy. That's why learners using this approach feel hopeful, energized, and self-motivated.

Implementation Tasks

I have heard that it takes up to twenty-one iterations to habituate. As a budding pianist, I call that a very conservative estimate. Therefore, the third type of learning task we use is an implementation task. This invites the learners to use the new KSAs in the learning environment, immediately. They implement them in the workshop, class, or session. This is done to get feedback on the learner's interpretation of the content, and also to offer the learner opportunity to practice.

Although we do not yet have a tested formula, I propose at least one implementation learning task for every input learning task. Consider the examples offered in this book so far; the task you read at the end of Chapter One is an implementation task.

REVIEWING THE IMPLEMENTATION TASK
FROM CHAPTER ONE

Examine the learning tasks you have been asked to do in this book so far. Consider how well they apply this definition: A learning task is an open question put to learners who have all the resources they need to respond.

Learning task 1: As you read this section on assumptions, consider what the opposite of each assumption involves.

Learning task 2: Read over these four assumptions. Describe for yourself what each might mean in your situation.

Assumption 1: Learners arrive with the capacity to do the work involved in learning.

Assumption 2: Learners learn when they are actively engaged with the content, cognitively, emotionally, and physically.

Assumption 3: New content can be presented through a learning task.

Assumption 4: Learning tasks lead to accountability and are habit forming.

Learning task 3: Examine this section on defining a learning task. What would you add to the definition?

These are all implementation tasks. An implementation task offers opportunity to review and integrate concepts, practice skills, and examine and practice new attitudes within the session, course, or class. The implementation task is an opportunity for assessment: Have they got it?

Iteration does not mean repetition, which can be tedious. I interpret *iteration* as a challenge to say and use the central concepts of a course hundreds of times, and always differently. The aesthetics of designing and leading effective learning tasks demands creative iteration.

Here is another example of an implementation task from the designs we have already examined. Do you remember this task from Chapter Two?

REVIEW OF IMPLEMENTATION TASK FROM CHAPTER TWO

E-mail learning task 3: Set up an account.

Task 3A: Make a decision and set up your own temporary account using one of the providers. Follow the setup steps. What are your questions?

Task 3B: Send me an e-mail at my address. Delete, or file, the e-mail you sent me. What are your questions?

This is an implementation task, practicing and reinforcing, within the class, a skill being learned. Once they have done this learning task and gotten feedback on their performance and responses to their questions, learners know that they know.

Integration Tasks

The final type of learning task is an integration task, where learners are invited to apply what they have learned to their life and work. This integration may be through a projection task that invites learners to imagine what integrating the new learning accomplishes in their workplace or life. It may be a learning task to be accomplished after the course or session, with a reporting element so that feedback can be offered.

In our programs teaching the design of adult learning, we invite learners to send designs to us for review and feedback. Their designing using what they learned in the weeklong "Learning to Listen, Learning to Teach" course *is* the integration task.

Integration tasks examine transfer, which is the use of new KSAs in the workplace or in life. If you do not structure integration tasks in a course or workshop session, it is less likely that the transfer will be explicit and intentional. Offering feedback on such tasks ensures not only that they are accomplished but also that the skills are reinforced at the same time. It is an ongoing opportunity for assessment, without being a testing task.

Integration learning tasks look to the future and often are designed to take place in the future. This is why it is vital to build a feedback mechanism into such learning tasks.

Task 8B: Differences

Describe the differences you see now between these four types of learning task: inductive work, input, implementation, and integration. (By the way, this is an implementation task, isn't it?)

As you practice designing these four types of learning task, you will no doubt be surprised to discover how creative you become.

What About Testing Tasks?

To a recent query about testing in an adult learning program, I responded, "Well, all my curves move upward. The grade is steep when you are teaching people facts for life. Adult learners themselves are the only ones who can measure personal success."

Sarah Gravett, my colleague in South Africa, has this to say in a recent e-mail about the potential of learning tasks for assessment: "Think of assessment not as something that takes place after learning but as a process that should take place continuously during teaching because one uses assessment to monitor student understanding and progress. Then one realizes that learning tasks are also assessment tasks. When the teacher invites the responses from the groups after engaging with the learning tasks, she can immediately gather whether students understand, and so can the students! I think that an important strength of learning tasks is indeed that they enable continuous assessment. Learning tasks are simultaneously assessment tasks!"

In a more formal setting, where tests are part of a system there is no reason a testing task cannot also be a learning task. If I were teaching a modern history course to adults, the test might be:

- Take Sunday's *New York Times* "News of the Week in Review."
- Select three articles, and for each write both a summary of the article and a background paragraph offering context data for the article. Also identify at least two reference books for each of the articles you selected.
- Use the Internet and those reference books to design your background paragraph.

In a basic chemistry course for adults, the test can be:

- Take the chart of the elements into your kitchen.
- Examine all the cleaning items under the sink, and at least two items from the refrigerator or pantry.
- Show which elements are active in those items.
- Write an honest advertisement for each of the household items you analyzed, telling buyers what they are getting in this item and how they should use it.

Can you see the potential of learning tasks as testing tasks? It is my hope that teachers of adults will get so creative in designing learning tasks that their creativity spills over into the testing arena.

Synthesis

In Chapter Four, we have examined in detail four types of learning task: inductive, input, implementation, and integration. In Chapter Five, we examine the verbs that work well in designing learning tasks.

5

The Power of Action: "The Verb's the Thing"

Learning Task 9

Peter Perkins is an educator who has been working for years with young adults in Vermont. He and his team design short courses and workshops for young adults on the subject of prevention. Prevention in this setting teaches how we can work ahead of trouble, making certain that young people never get to stand in front of a judge.

Perkins had some very exciting content to teach. He needed to organize it and design learning tasks that would engage these young people fully. This content was, for them, a matter of life and death.

Perkins loves to describe the change in response that he saw when he moved from presentations about learning and job possibilities to action tasks for the learners. He had always set up the objectives of their courses in the way he was taught, using outcomes-based objectives ("Participants will be able to . . . ," "Participants will learn . . . ," "Participants will know. . . ."). He knew that we teach as we were taught; he realized that we design as we were designed for.

After working with the JUBILEE Popular Education Center, Perkins and the Vermont Youth Project team set up courses with challenging and demanding learning tasks that used verbs calling for accountable performance during the session ("Participants will *name* two examples of risky behavior," "Participants will *design* a personal program," "Participants will *write* a job application). As Perkins declared, "The verb's the thing!"

Learning Task 9: The Verb's the Thing!

Task 9A: Examine these two sets of learning tasks. Identify the differences you perceive.

LEARNING TASKS, SET ONE

VERB LEARNING TASK 1 (DOW JONES AVERAGE)

Learn the names of the thirty companies represented in the Dow Jones industrial average. What are the norms for selection to the Dow?

VERB LEARNING TASK 2 (DOW JONES AVERAGE)

Task 1: On the Internet, read the history of the Dow Jones average. How is the DJIA useful to the global economy?

Task 2: Choose two companies included in the Dow Jones average. On the Internet, trace the history of their stock over the past four years. Also on the Internet, read the histories of these companies.

Task 3: Decide why each was selected for the Dow Jones average.

LEARNING TASKS, SET TWO

VERB LEARNING TASK 1 (USING MICROSOFT POWERPOINT)

Design a presentation on a topic of your choice, using Microsoft PowerPoint. Use the help menu for instructions and guidance.

VERB LEARNING TASK 2 (USING MICROSOFT POWERPOINT)

Task 1: Launch Microsoft PowerPoint. Open the File menu and select New; in the dialog box, choose the Presentations tab; select AutoContent Wizard.

Task 2: Work through the steps to design a slide presentation.

Task 3: Change the view of your slide presentation using the icons on the lower left corner near the bottom of the screen.

Task 4: Use *each* of the icons on the main page of Power-Point to edit one page of your slide presentation.

Task 5: Print and post one of your slides. Explain to your small group how you got that appearance.

Differences

In both of the first learning tasks, the verbs were general. In both of the second learning tasks, the verbs were specific. To design learning tasks, specific is better than general.

The sequence of steps is laid out in the second learning tasks. If the sequence is not explicit in the design, learners can be confused by a task that is not just general but too big to try.

Our familiarity with computer programming gives us an edge in designing learning tasks. A useful program tutorial for software is a well-sequenced series of learning tasks with a great deal of electronic structure and support.

Examine the verbs in the sets of learning tasks. Notice we do not use *learn* or *understand*. *Learn* is what we call a "huge verb"; it is too big for a learning task. *Understand* is a similar huge verb, too big for a single learning task. *Learn* (along with the implied verb *understand*) is the goal of the event. This approach to adult learning holds that we learn through an active process, through doing something with that we are learning. *Learn* therefore is not in itself an active verb. Active verbs in learning tasks are tough, specific, and respectful.

In set two, the verbs *design* and *use* are strong and specific. However, here they are in a context that is too broad to be functional. It does not help a learner to say "Use the dictionary to find the right word" or "Use the thesaurus to find the appropriate phrase." Our task as educators is to narrow those parameters so that learners can take small steps toward significant learning.

In 1956, Benjamin Bloom and a group of colleagues gave those of us who are keen on using learning tasks a great gift. They categorized verbs by their learning domain: cognitive, affective, or psychomotor.

Task 9B: Examine the list of verbs in Table 5.1, categorized by learning domain. What verbs would you add?

As you prepare achievement-based objectives and learning tasks, consider using the verbs on this list.

In *Problem Based Learning and Other Curriculum Models for the Multiple Intelligences Classroom*, Fogarty suggests another set of categories (Table 5.2).

However, not all the verbs on these lists necessarily make effective learning tasks. What verbs make a great learning task?

Tough Verbs. By *tough verbs* I mean verbs that demand considered action, verbs that challenge a learner to stretch and grow. *Design, edit, decide, select, write, distinguish x from y, illustrate, organize, solve, resolve,* and *realign* are examples of what I call tough verbs. You can run, but you can't hide from these verbs; they do not allow pedantic play or abstract meandering.

Productive Verbs. You want verbs in your learning tasks that *produce* for your learners—verbs such as *list, design, compose, write, prepare, reorganize, select, develop, diagram, illustrate,* and so on. These verbs produce, and the products are indicators of the learning that is taking place. With productive verbs at work, assessment of learning is immediate.

One of the verbs I avoid in learning tasks is *discuss*. The reason I do not use it is that there is no product of *discuss*; it can go on and on. It does not have the exhilarating immediacy in a learning task of verbs demanding a product, such as *design, create, list*.

Respectful Verbs. The verbs you select as the engines of your learning tasks must fit the *who*, the particular group of learners for

TABLE 5.1 Bloom's Set of Verbs.

Cognitive	Affective	Psychomotor
Select	Revise	Design
Define	Edit	Operate
Identify	Share	Set Up
List	Respond To	Practice
Name	Approve	Organize
State	Put in Priority Order	Exhibit
Compare	Acclaim	Review
Distinguish	Brag	Recite
Contrast	Applaud	Play
Read	Assist	Diagram
Demonstrate	Protest	Draw
Relate	Agree	Compose
Group	Change	Realign
Estimate	Debate	Affix
Reflect	Support	Put
Solve	Deny	Take
Employ	Comply with	Write
Complete	Control	Prepare
Classify	Listen to	Dramatize
Apply	Accept	Build
Illustrate	Celebrate	Choose
Synthesize	Reframe	Manipulate
Analyze	Choose	Redesign
Design	Value	Rearrange
Edit	Prefer	Employ
Add	Enjoy	
Delete	Rank	
Examine	Resist	
Organize	Evaluate	
Change	Notice	
Develop	Relate to	
Review		
Diagnose		

Source: Piskurich (1993), pp. 66–67.

TABLE 5.2 Verbs Categorized by Multiple Intelligence.

Verbal	Visual	Logical	Musical	Interpersonal	Intrapersonal	Bodily	Naturalist
Report	Design a story	Reason	Sing	Discuss	Journal	Dance	Relate
Paraphrase	Paint	Collect	Listen	Respond	Intuit	Sculpt	Discover
Write	Draw	Record	Compose	Dialogue	Reflect	Perform	Uncover
Joke	Observe	Analyze	Audiotape	Report	Log	Prepare	Observe
Create	Illustrate	Graph	Improvise	Survey	Mediate	Construct	Dig
Label	Diagram	Compare	Select music	Question	Study	Act	Plant
Recite	Depict	Contrast	Critique music	Paraphrase	Rehearse	Role-play	Design
Listen	Show	Rank		Clarify	Self-assemble	Dramatize	Compare
List		Evaluate		Affirm	Express	Pantomime	Display
Retell		Sort				Sort	

Source: From *Problem-Based Learning and Other Curriculum Models for the Multiple Intelligences Classroom* by Robin Fogarty, © 1997 IRI/SkyLight Training and Publishing, Inc. Adapted with permission of SkyLight Professional Development, Arlington Heights, IL.

whom you are designing. This concern for the appropriate verb is a sign of respect for your learners. Push the young adults to a grunting, steaming, sweaty level of learning by using challenging, tough verbs; urge the grandparents by gentle verbs to stretch beyond their limits; stimulate patients in a clinical setting to overcome their present disabilities by asking for encouraging, well-sequenced verbs.

Task 9C: Look back at any one of the eight learning tasks offered in this book so far, and examine one learning task in the various sample designs. What do you notice about the verbs that were used?

CIPP (Context, Input, Process, Product)

The CIPP concept, described by Sara Steele in a chapter in the *Handbook of Adult and Continuing Education* (Merriam and Cunningham, 1989), can be of use to designers here. CIPP stands for context, input, process, and product. It was first proposed as a model for four basic areas of programmatic decisions; it identifies key aspects of programs that should be considered in relation to each other.

Context. This relates to the *who*, *why*, *when*, and *where* of the seven steps of planning. The verbs you choose are designed to relate gracefully to the context. You do not invite (*who*) emeritus physicians to climb a wall, or challenge youthful physician's assistants to analyze a specific and complicated case study for a diagnosis. The verb must fit the context.

The situation (*why*) is considered so as to select verbs for the learning tasks that are immediate to that situation. *When* and *where* control the kinds of verb you can use in terms of time frame and site.

Input. In the CIPP model, input refers to the resources needed to teach. I see it relating both to the content (*what*) and the achievement-based objectives (*what for*). If you are teaching PowerPoint, for example, certainly each learner must have immediate access to that program to learn and practice using it. The elements of the program are your specific designated content, not the aggregate PowerPoint program, which is too large to handle in a learning task.

Since the achievement-based objectives (*what for*) are what the learners do with the content (*what*), tough, productive, and respectful verbs come in here. A well-wrought achievement-based objective uses effective verbs; for example, "By the end of this session, all participants will have *identified* and *used* all the icons on the main screen of PowerPoint."

Can you see how such an achievement-based objective differs from a goal such as "learn PowerPoint"? Goals are general. Goals can use broad and general verbs (*learn, understand, enhance, improve*, and so on). Achievement-based objectives must sparkle with specificity, since they lead directly to a set of learning tasks.

Process. Process in the CIPP model relates to the learning task, which includes sharing and evaluating the products from the learning task. It is, in fact, the *how* of the seven steps of planning.

Product. As we have said, the product of an effective learning task demonstrates the learning and shows to teacher and learners alike all that has been achieved and learned. They know that they know when they can point to the practical, useful products of their learning tasks.

A thesis or dissertation is a product of graduate study that proves to the man or woman and to the world that he or she is indeed a master of the discipline. A portfolio of self-designed recipes using the principles of nutrition for health is a product that enables a learner to say he or she knows how to design meals for a healthy family.

If you design an effective learning session, in which the seven elements of learners, situation, time, site, content, objectives, and learning tasks fit together well, you can be assured of accountable learning. That is, learners achieve those objectives by doing learning tasks that teach the content in such a way that they can say, "We know that we know." The verb is indeed the thing.

Task 9D: Having read the description of the CIPP model, name one way it differs from the seven steps of planning and the use of learning tasks.

Synthesis

In Chapter Five, we have explored the qualities of verbs that we need for effective learning tasks. We have looked at two sets of categorized verbs and examined some criteria to determine which verbs are best for learning tasks. We have related the CIPP model (context, input, process, and product) to the seven steps of planning. In Chapter Six, we examine another program that teaches some principles and practices to guide the design of appropriate learning tasks.

learning tasks.

6

Principles to Guide Design

Learning Task 10

Some years ago, I was invited to work with the medical team
at a major United Nations organization to design their annual
health education program. As part of our contract, I interviewed
numerous doctors and health education specialists about the state
of the department and its projects. The information I gleaned
through this needs assessment helped me design a program that I
sent to the medical program director for review.

The draft was accepted, and we got to work. Forty medical staff
from around the world gathered for a three-day session to examine
their present health education programs, and to redesign them
where necessary.

As we began, using learning tasks to warm up, review the program, and identify personal expectations, one of the senior staff
people objected. He had reviewed the program but was not aware
from that design how radical a departure it would be from their
usual series of lectures on medical or strategic topics. To this physician, the idea of all participants working as relatively equal members of the session, in small groups, was appalling. He called for a
special meeting with the medical program director, some of his
peers, and me at lunchtime.

In that meeting, the decision was made to abandon this design
and move to inviting senior members to offer their views on present

issues and local problem areas. The afternoon was a series of such presentations.

I was extraneous under the new arrangement and sat quietly, observing. Late the first night, I received a call at my hotel. It was the director. She had been doing some serious political action, working with caucus after caucus, and finally had made a decision: "We are going back to our original design. We want you to lead it tomorrow." "Very well," I said.

The next morning we took up where we had left off. The doctor who initiated the rebellion was sitting rather stiffly at one table, somewhat aloof and distant. But the learning task must have engaged him because within fifteen minutes his suit jacket was draped over the chair, his white shirt sleeves were rolled up, and he was leading his table in completing an analysis of annual data and drawing conclusions that would shape the new programs.

From across the room, the medical program director caught my eye. She too saw the transformation in our critic and smiled at me knowingly.

Resistance to this new approach is not only to be expected but also to be celebrated. This doctor was wise enough to know that the revolution in educational process was a sign of a deeper change in organizational design and operation. Such change is threatening—and necessary, as the agency (like all of us) moves into a global economy.

If you have read *Training Through Dialogue* (Vella, 1995), you may recall the description of fifty principles and practices for accountable learning. All of these are at play in an effective learning task. Since learning tasks implement achievement-based objectives, they are naturally relevant to the purpose of the program. And since the learning task is an open question, it can show respect for the perspective of each learner as subject of his or her own learning. A learning task engages learners in action and reflection. The design of a learning task must challenge learners cognitively and emotionally—and often challenge them to complete some psychomotor activity. The safety of the learner is correlated to the challenge of the learning task.

During a needs assessment, the designer of a program can see and hear what kinds of learning task a group needs and wants. If the program addresses real needs, the learning task has immediacy. A learning task invites dialogue between learner and teacher and among learners as well. Learning tasks are frequently designed to be accomplished in a small group, moving from individual work to pairs to work in a larger group. Such small-group work affords opportunity for inclusion, allowing each individual to work in his or her own learning style. It allows us to celebrate the autonomy of each learner.

When a learning task invites stories from life, or action as a group followed by reflection, it uses the principle of praxis; this is an inductive approach. Another route is moving from theory to practice, the deductive approach. Both make for useful learning tasks.

New content is analyzed through a learning task; then, at the end of a class, course, or session, there is a synthesis task, putting it all together. The sequence of learning tasks, from simple to complex, from easy to difficult, offers constant reinforcement of learning. At the outset, a warm-up is a learning task to focus the group on the topic. At the end, a force-field analysis can be used to identify what was most useful in the learning, and what might be done differently in the process next time. Throughout, the skillful educator uses silence to allow learners to consider their input, and to work on their team projects. Affirmation of their effort and of the products of their learning tasks is basic to this approach.

Content is presented through printed materials, overheads, case studies, and lectures, with appropriate learning tasks to engage learners in analyzing or editing the content. Each learning task, and the program as a whole, has a title.

Learning Task 10: Principles and Practices at Work

This learning task demonstrates how the principles and practices can work.

Task 10A

Examine this excerpt from the design of a course in adult learning theory. You may already have seen a version of this course design in *Training Through Dialogue*. At this point, we are using it to discover the principles and practices at work. Circle or note all of the principles and practices you see in the four selected learning tasks.

LEARNING TO LISTEN, LEARNING TO TEACH

THE SEVEN STEPS OF PLANNING

1. *Who* (participants): ten adult educators who work in training and adult education.
2. *Why* (the situation): these educators need to find a sure way to design and do their adult education programs.
3. *When*: five days (thirty hours).
4. *Where*: a room with a circle of chairs and tables for three or four people at a table. The room is equipped with a VCR and monitor, a CD and audiocassette player, two easels, flipcharts, and a table for the two staff.
5. *What* (content, KSAs): content dealt with in the selected learning tasks is marked with an asterisk. Note that the content is a set of nouns.

   *Adult learning theory

   *Problem-posing approach (dialogue); the "banking" approach (monologue)

   Lewin's dozen principles for learning

   Respect, use of lavish affirmation

   Berne's theory of communications, achievement-based objectives

   *Accountability, engagement, immediacy, design of a learning event

   Seven steps of planning

   How to use a video clip

How to design and use a warm-up

*Feedback: getting it and giving it

Design of problem-posing learning materials

How to design and use open questions

How to design an effective chart

Effective ways of working in small groups

Group and task maintenance in small groups: how groups work

How to do a learning needs assessment

*Generative themes of a group

Consultative and deliberative voices

Safety in the learning situation

Subject: the learner as decision maker

Learning, transfer, and impact (evaluation concepts)

6. *What for* (achievement-based objectives): note that these objectives are quantifiable and verifiable; therefore, we are accountable to achieve them! All of these achievement-based objectives are implemented through a design that models this problem-posing approach, that demonstrates the use of all the skills, knowledge, and attitudes being taught. Note too that the achievement-based objectives begin with verbs; this indicates what the learner will do with what is being learned.

By the end of this five-day course, all participants will have

- Reviewed current adult learning theory

- Distinguished between monologue ("banking") and dialogue (problem-posing) as approaches to learning (Freire's concept)

- Reviewed basic communications theory using Berne's paradigm (transactional analysis: parent, adult, child)

- Practiced doing a learning needs assessment

- Identified generative themes of a group
- Practiced working in small groups
- Examined a theory of how groups work
- Used and evaluated all the principles and practices of adult learning
- Practiced designing and using open questions
- Practiced designing learning sessions in teams (meetings, courses, workshops, orientation programs, training sessions), using the principles and practices
- Practiced designing warm-ups that are learning tasks
- Used found objects in a warm-up
- Examined a video clip and identified ways to use it effectively
- Designed, and named the qualities of, an effective chart
- Practiced teaching using their own design
- Practiced learning as subjects (decision makers) of their own learning
- Reviewed theory on feedback, and practiced giving and getting feedback on designs and teaching
- Examined a model for planning (the four I's)
- Identified learning, transfer, and impact (concepts in evaluation)
- Named resources in adult learning: books, journals, professional organizations, courses, etc.

7. *How*: learning tasks and materials (the program). Note that we do what we are learning. We model what we are teaching.

THE PROGRAM
DAY ONE
9:00 A.M. Welcome

COURSE TASK 1 Warm-up. To get to know one another and to share in the large group, please select a found object that symbolizes your work in this world. Share your symbols and something about yourself in pairs. Then, we'll hear from all of you.

COURSE TASK 2 Program review, objectives, and our expectations. Listen to the achievement-based objectives for this week-long course, and the topical program for each day. At your table, tell your own personal expectations, that is, what you hope to do or learn by Friday at 3:00 P.M.

Then write these on Post-it notes, using felt pens, putting one on each note. Initial each expectation. We'll hear all of them.

COURSE TASK 3 How adults learn.

Task 3A: In pairs, describe the best learning situation you have ever experienced in your life. Then analyze it. Name the factors that made it so good. Write these factors on Post-it notes, one on each note. Post them. We'll share all your factors and then compare them with some current research on adult learning, which you will find on chart three.

Task 3B: Respect (Knowles's prime factor). Read these notes on respect, and circle what you see is most useful to you. We'll hear a sampling.

SHOWING RESPECT When asking participants to report back from a task, avoid using the round-robin approach in which you go from one participant to another around the table or around the room. Adults are decision makers and subjects of their own learning; they are capable of deciding for themselves whether and when they want to speak. Teachers can show respect by allowing participants to decide for themselves, by asking "Who wishes to respond?" Do not call attention to someone who has passed. By asking, you can ensure that everyone who wants to speak has the opportunity. If you do notice a participant passing on several occasions, a private conversation to learn why is appropriate.

Task 3C: In your table group, describe how you show respect to the adults you work with or teach. What results have you seen from such explicit respect? We'll share a sample of results.

Task 3D: Learners as subjects or decision makers. Listen to this lecture, reading along as you listen.

SUBJECTS OF THEIR OWN LEARNING Adults are required by daily life to be decision makers. They generally expect to be treated as such. We all resist being treated as objects. To be treated as a subject means being honored for our years of experience and our ability to make decisions. Treating participants of a learning session as subjects of their own learning, as decision makers, is a major principle in accountable learning. The learning is in the doing and in the deciding. Teachers must be careful not to steal learning opportunities from adult learners by making decisions for them!

Task 3E: In your table group, describe what it feels like to be the subject of your own learning. What did you see us do this morning to indicate that we view you as the subject of your own learning?

COURSE TASK 4 Generative themes of a group. Read this short explanation of generative themes of a group. What are your questions?

GENERATIVE THEMES Generative themes are those ideas and issues, problems and joys that people talk about, worry about, and celebrate. They can be specific for a particular time and season, or general. A grandmother, for example, will readily tell you about her generative theme: her new grandson! A woman whose husband has lost his job manifests her generative theme in the way she walks and the look on her face; she is worried, and depressed! Near examination time, a student is nervous, talks quickly, is irritable at home, and finds himself drinking a lot. His generative theme is the exam!

Why generative themes? These ideas, problems, joys, and issues generate energy. When we do a learning needs assessment, we search for the generative themes of the learners so that we might address them in our design. Freire uses the term in his book *Pedagogy of the Oppressed*: "Actually, themes exist in people in their relations with the world, with reference to concrete facts" (1993, p. 87).

Task 4A: At your table, identify some of the themes you have heard in this group so far. Write them on note cards, and offer one or two from each table. We'll share a sample of themes.

Task 4B: On day three, you will design together to teach us. Tell one way you see the themes of this group informing your designs.

In addition to application of the principles and practices, this excerpt showed you the connection among learning tasks (*how*), the named content (*what*), and the achievement-based objectives (*what for*) of the course.

Task 10B

Here is a checklist of principles and practices. At the end of the checklist, write the questions you would add to it.

☐ How is the learning task you are designing congruent with the content you are teaching?

☐ How have you used case studies, stories, video clips, or found objects to invite reflection on learners' life and work?

☐ How have you interchanged inductive work (starting with life) and deductive work (starting with theory)?

☐ What kind of preparation have you done for this program?

☐ Are all the learning tasks designed with enough challenge and intensity to keep up the energy needed to learn?

☐ Have you carefully titled each learning task?

☐ Is there a warm-up learning task to get them into the program?

☐ Is there a learning task inviting their expectations, the results of which can be used at the end to formulate feedback and offer evaluation indicators?

☐ Do you have a significant synthesis and closure task?

☐ In terms of leading the learning tasks, how well are you using thanks, affirmation, paraphrasing, and echoing?

☐ How do you manage time so that all the learning tasks in a program are completed?

☐ How do you use charts to show relations and connections? How do you use charts and overhead projections to set and record tasks?

☐ How do you assure learners that we are working toward their learning with autonomy?

☐ How well do you work toward inclusion?

☐ How well do you use humor?

☐ Do all the learning tasks have titles?

☐ Does the entire program have a title?

☐ Describe the ways you have identified to track transfer and indicate impact

☐ _____

☐ _____

As you can see, such a checklist of questions clarifies and informs your design. Learning tasks are effective insofar as they incorporate these principles and practices for accountable learning.

Synthesis

In this chapter, we have reviewed some of the principles and practices of this learning-centered approach and examined a checklist of questions to ensure that all the principles and practices are considered as we design and teach. In Chapter Seven, we look at theories and practices to guide us as we lead learning tasks and work with diverse learners.

7

The Art of Leading Learning Tasks

Learning Tasks 11 and 12

Fernando Menendez (whom we met in Chapter Four) and I were leading the "Learning to Listen, Learning to Teach" course in Durham, North Carolina, some years ago. He and I worked well together, and we took great pride in that. On the third day of the course, we suddenly had to change rooms at the center. After we got everyone into the new room, I led the learning task on how to use a video clip.

At the break after the learning task, I smiled at Fernando and said, "Well, in spite of everything, that task went well!"

"Yes, it did, Jane. However, I was supposed to have led it!"

Our assiduous preparation for the course did not prevent my stepping up to bat out of turn. I thanked my partner for his gracious forgiveness and resolved to be more attentive to details such as who is leading which task.

Learning Task 11: Skills for Leading Learning Tasks

Examine this checklist of skills. "Grade" yourself with this 5-point scale:

1. Yes, I do this all the time.
2. I need to pay attention to this.

3. I need to ask for feedback on this.

4. I'm not sure what this means.

5. Help!

SKILLS FOR LEADING LEARNING TASKS: A CHECKLIST

Every time I design and teach, I make sure that I

☐ Prepare each learning task

☐ Walk through it with my partner

☐ Prepare materials (charts, pens, post-it notes, tape)

☐ Set the task clearly, by reading it

☐ Set the end time

☐ Ask the learners, "Is the task clear?"

☐ Sit still, keep quiet, and pay attention as they work

☐ Keep time

☐ Invite large-group sharing

☐ Welcome responses

☐ Echo, paraphrase, and affirm

☐ Summarize the task

☐ Make a smooth transition to the next task

☐ Keep eye contact with my partner, and with the participants

☐ Set lots of breaks

☐ Set an end time for breaks

☐ Clean up for the next task

☐ Use silence to get attention

☐ Laugh a lot

☐ Keep relevant notes for a course report

☐ Affirm difficult input with a simple thank-you

Task 11A: What would you add to this list of skills?

☐ _____

☐ _____

Task 11B: Mark those on which you scored 3, 4, or 5. You will want to practice these as you teach using learning tasks.

Leading learning tasks takes skill, and also a modicum of humility. The teacher, in setting and leading the learning tasks, is on center stage. What she is doing is what she is teaching. Although the discrete skills in the checklist seem facile, they indicate a generous attitude and willing spirit. If these skills are used consistently, they demonstrate a graceful and practical art. In the next section, we examine each item on the checklist in detail.

Prepare Each Learning Task

In the design stage, the teacher uses the seven steps of planning to compose a complete design. At the *how* step, each learning task is thoughtfully prepared. The teacher needs to know the purpose of each task, its place in the sequence of tasks, and its direction (whether toward reflection or action). If you are working with a coteacher, it is vital that you both know your particular responsibility in each learning task. This preparation involves thorough research on the content, to be sure that learning tasks contain substantive input.

Walk Through It with My Partner

Even if you are not teaching with another, walk through a learning task with a partner, to make sure the directions are clear, the sequence comprehensible, and the product tangible. You will be surprised what you discover in such a dress rehearsal. Learning tasks are dialogues. Practice is helpful, to test how viable the dialogue is.

Prepare Materials

Having charts, pens, note cards, handouts, and video clips is a vital aspect of using learning tasks. When you put learners to work, they must have the tools of their trade at hand. Here is another argument for having a coteacher, who can be responsible for materials while you are in charge of leading the task. Video clips must be previewed and cued to play exactly where and when you want them to begin. Obviously, do not give out materials while you are setting a learning task; if you do so, people turn to read any new material handed to them and they do not listen to the directions. Timing is vital here. A crisp system for distributing materials at the appropriate moment keeps energy up for learning.

Set the Learning Task Clearly

Reading the learning task as it is written in the course material seems a simple enough task. However, we have seen teachers try to set the task by heart, without using the coursebook or chart. This often leads to confusion. Read the task as it is written.

Language is important here. When I hear teachers say, "Now, I want you to—" I cringe. The appropriate way to set a learning task for adults who know they are respected as autonomous learners is, very simply, to say, "The next learning task is. . . ."

Set the End Time

Every learning task has a time frame. Again, I do not like hearing teachers say, "I'll give you thirty minutes for this task." The appropriate thing is to set the end time ("We'll share your work at 8:50," or " We'll see where you are at 9:15"). Setting the end time raises energy among the learners. They know they have a job to do and must show the product by 9:15. In Chapter Eight, we consider multiple aspects of timing in this approach to accountable learning. However, it is important to remember that the shorter the time to get a job done, the higher the energy of the learners. The decision on a time frame for each learning task is made while designing the whole program. Be crisp and clear in setting the end time, and do not change it unless you absolutely must. Learners will let you know if you have indeed underestimated the time they need to get a learning task done.

Ask the Learners, "Is the Task Clear?"

Used after setting each task, this short phrase gives learners the opportunity to say, "No, not yet." We have all seen a group start working and then they look at one another until someone asks, "What are we supposed to be doing?" We can avoid this situation with a simple closed question: "Is the task clear?" This is a great way to show respect to adult learners.

Sit Still, Keep Quiet, and Pay Attention

Here's a new role for the professor. When learners are deeply engaged in a learning task, the teacher's role is to sit still, keep quiet, and pay attention. I feel very strongly about not intervening in a group without invitation to do so from a group member or members. The learning place is sacred. Men and women need to feel their autonomy; they need to struggle with new content and skills long enough. We are not helpers. When invited, we offer a response to the questions asked, and then we leave. This is a new role indeed!

Keep Time

A major role for educators in this approach to accountable learning is timekeeper. We urge teachers to be faithful to the time frame (end time) set at the beginning of the learning task. We usually name the exact time to invite learners to complete a task ("It is now 9:10. That means we have five minutes before 9:15, when we will share your results"). Compare that with "Hurry up now, it's time!" or "Are you nearly finished?"

Less-than-accurate timekeeping means less accountable learning. Crisp, clear definition of the time frame adds to the possibility of accountable learning.

Welcome Responses

Once a learning task has been completed, the teacher sits and, in a relaxed manner, asks, "Who wants to share?" Avoid round-robin sharing, where one person (or group representative) goes after another in a preset fashion. Never choose for learners what they can choose for themselves.

Your job as teacher is to welcome these responses, affirm the efforts involved in developing them, correct and confirm, and add your experience and research to their findings. This is a chance for your input in a dialogue initiated by the learning task. In my experience, this is the occasion for learners' recreating and reconstituting the content to suit their context.

Invite Large-Group Sharing

When responses are to be presented or products shared, it is time for the large group to enter the dialogue. Now your leadership role is not unlike that of a conductor of a symphony orchestra, bringing in people as they wish to add their thoughts or questions, responding to questions and adding new information, and building the knowledge or skill together.

Echo, Paraphrase, and Affirm

Affirmation by echoing or paraphrasing what one person says, or what a group reports, is a powerful aid to learning. Imagine how a learner feels when the professor says, "Am I to understand that you mean . . . ? Well, that's a unique interpretation. I've never thought of that myself. Well done!"

Echoing means you repeat exactly what the learners have said. Paraphrasing is just that: you repeat their thoughts in a shortened or different form. In any case, such keen listening is rewarded by keen learning.

Summarize the Task

At some point, the dialogue must be summarized. This is your job: "Well, we have decided that . . ." or "Now, we have realized how. . . ." Such a synthesis is a cue to move to the next learning task in the sequence. This is another place where your experience and knowledge can be gracefully brought in ("What we have just learned is laid out very clearly in [the text], which you might want to review" or "What we just learned was summed up by _____, when he said . . .").

Make a Smooth Transition to the Next Task

Your summary and synthesis leads to the next learning task and also enables the learners to see the course or session as a whole. I am always explicit about the connections between learning tasks ("Having completed this task, we are ready, after a ten-minute break, to take on the next learning task . . .").

Keep Eye Contact with My Partner and with the Participants

In all of this—welcoming the response of a small group or an individual, inviting response and creative work from the large group— eye contact is vital. Always look directly at the speaker; this is an aspect of good listening. At the same time, keep occasional eye contact with your teaching partner so that her needs are met and she can cue you into something she has noticed.

Set Lots of Breaks

In courses or workshop sessions, we take a short break after each learning task. This serves to raise energy and invites excited sharing on the learning that is taking place. Sometimes it is important to change the makeup of the small groups. This can take place during a break, before beginning a new learning task. Obviously, such a decision depends on the structure and purpose of the learning event.

Set an End Time for the Break

When setting breaks, also set an end time. Rather than "We'll take a fifteen-minute break," say, "We'll start learning task number five at 10:30 sharp." Can you hear the difference?

Clean Up for the Next Task

While learners are on their short break, teachers can sort out what is needed for the next learning task, set up for it, and clear away the debris created in the previous task. The more gracefully this house-keeping takes place, the more coherent are all the actions toward accountable learning.

Use Silence to Get Attention

When learning tasks are challenging and engaging, small groups can get very noisy—or intensely quiet—in their involvement. Rather than calling out loud for attention, try standing silently, within sight of all learners. After a few seconds, learners will fall silent, waiting for you to speak.

Laugh a Lot

The more relaxed and confident you are as a leader of intense and difficult learning tasks, the more relaxed and confident learners are.

One way to project that attitude is through genuine and spontaneous laughter.

Keep Relevant Notes for a Course Report

This is an important role for any teacher. A course or workshop report serves as a useful reminder for the learners, a valuable evaluation instrument for the designers and teachers, and useful documentation for funders. It is easier to gather data incrementally during a session, learning task by learning task, than to recreate the event at the end. Therefore, in a long course I try to write the report day by day.

Affirm Difficult Input with a Simple Thank-You

This system of dialogue opens the way for difficult input from learners, some of whom may be disgruntled or angry. Never get into a verbal shouting match with a learner. One way to diffuse such an event is for you, as teacher, to say thank-you: "Thank you for making clear how this is affecting you. Let me see what we can do later to deal with this."

Envisioning Enhanced Learning

Imagine your next course. See yourself designing and using learning tasks and doing all the actions on that checklist. Identify one way using learning tasks enhances your teaching and their learning.

Different Forms of Questions

The open question is central to the design of learning tasks.

Learning Task 12: Three Levels of Questions

Consider these three levels of questioning for design and teaching. What other levels would you add to this list?

Level One: Epistemological Questions

Epistemological questions deal with those principles and practices at a level of transcendence that applies to all educational events. In any culture or with any group, the teacher must prepare the content, engage the learners, put the material into an appropriate sequence, design for reinforcement, and allow adequate time for the content to be worked through. The checklist in this chapter reflects these principles and practices.

Level Two: Categorical Questions

Categorical questions address the differences involved in working with diverse categories of learners: lawyers, doctors, senior citizens, youth, etc. Depending on the program, it should be clear that learning tasks appropriate for young military recruits might not be appropriate for a group of their grandfathers in a senior center.

Level Three: Personal Questions

Learning styles are idiosyncratic and personal. Even as we review our designs and learning tasks to be certain that we are inclusive of all learning styles, we know we cannot overlook any of the level-one and level-two questions.

We propose that effective teaching always involves consideration of level-one matters. Our concern for level-two (categorical) or level-three (personal) issues cannot preclude concern for basic principles of learning.

For example, a professor can be tempted to shape his content to the idiosyncratic needs and learning styles of the individuals in his class. Or a trainer can be tempted to change his program because a group of executives is too busy to give adequate time for the work. This theory suggests that such level-two and level-three (categorical or personal) concerns must come *after* we ask level-one questions. If epistemological phenomena are disregarded, we pay the price in diminished learning.

Here are some examples of questions at the three levels:

- These are busy executives. How much time can they spend in this course? (level two)

- This young man clearly learns best if material is presented visually. How can we make printed materials in this program less text-based? (level three)

- The learning tasks in this program are all cognitive. How can we get more affective and psychomotor tasks into the mix? (level one)

- This program is made up entirely of lectures. How can we put engaging learning tasks into it? (level one)

If a training or educational program fails, it is often because designers or leaders have avoided asking level-one questions because of situations controlled by level-two or level-three questions. If educational programs are successful with diverse groups, it is likely that the epistemological questions were seriously considered first, and then categorical and personal issues were addressed.

Synthesis

In Chapter Seven, we have examined a checklist of skills needed to lead learning tasks well. We have read an explanation of each skill and considered how all of them are involved in the art of leading learning tasks. We have examined the theory of three levels of questions, which can help us decide what kinds of learning task and which skills are appropriate for different groups of learners. In Chapter Eight, we look at the prime issue of time in using learning tasks.

8

Time and the Learning Task

Learning Task 13

I was invited by a major industry in the Research Triangle of North Carolina to design and lead a program with executives, on Peter Senge's challenging concept of the learning organization (1990). I saw this opportunity for our small company as a door opening into a major industry.

My colleague and I struggled to design a significant program for these busy executives, who offered us two hours of their very expensive time. Senge would, I trust, blanch at the idea of his enormous body of research being offered in that time frame.

We did get some time with the twenty executives on the phone for a needs assessment. We discovered through these conversations that all, to a man (sic!), were dubious of this enterprise. They felt their company had a singular product for the global market. They did not see why they had to look at their corporation as a learning organization.

We designed using the seven steps of planning, but our concern to share everything in Senge's work with these men won out over our experience and knowledge of timing. We selected six content items from Senge's text for our *what*. This led to six achievement-based objectives (*what for*) and seven learning tasks (*how*).

The course was a masterful design for a five- or six-hour session; 1ad two hours. But in spite of their initial reluctance, these men waded into the first learning tasks with gusto and energy. They sucked each bone of content dry, challenged Senge and us, and projected realistic and critical applications of what they were learning onto the company's structure and processes. At the end of one hour and forty-five minutes, we had successfully completed only three of the six learning tasks. To this day, I am embarrassed to confess that we simply had too much *what* for the *when*.

Too Much Time? Too Little?

Time has proven to be the most important factor in designing an effective learning task. If too much time is offered for any single task, energy drops, distractions abound, and both the product and the learning suffer. If too little time is afforded for any single learning task, learners are frustrated. Again, both product and learning suffer. How can we estimate the precise amount of time necessary for an effective learning task?

Ingredients

The guidelines proposed here have three essential ingredients: number of learners (N), time available (T), and content to be learned (C). These are the three elements to consider: N, C, and T.

Number of Learners (N). It takes more time to complete a learning task with a larger number of participants than with a smaller number. Although this sounds self-evident, it needs to be said. Consider the number of participants when you are deciding how long a session will take.

Even if men and women are working in small groups, "publishing" their results calls for more time with more groups. There is a wider dialogue with a larger number of people.

Time Available (T). At conferences or classes in a university or college setting, time is measured with a small dropper. A fifty-minute class or session is considered usual. Adult learning sessions often use the same framework. Many times we cannot control the time offered us; we can however, control what we do in it.

If we have the leisure of a one-day or a multiple-day course, we can include lengthy learning tasks. If we have to work in a tight time frame, the time for learning tasks is naturally limited. The principle to use here is relentless: at least one learning task for every achievement-based objective, and one achievement-based objective for every piece of content.

Therefore, if the time frame is limited, the content must be limited. The number of objectives is limited by the time frame. Our role as adult educators is not to "cover" a set of content, but to design and teach for accountable learning.

Content to Be Learned (C). The time for a learning task differs depending on whether it is new material learners are dealing with or content for review or synthesis. Initial work with new content naturally takes more time. Cognitive tasks, affective tasks, and psychomotor learning tasks differ in their time demands.

Allocating Time

Using this guideline—N (number of learners), T (total time allotted), and C (content)—you can see how to come to some allocation of time per learning task. For example, in Chapter Six we examined four learning tasks set in a weeklong course for ten adult educators. Here, N = ten, C = new material, and T = thirty hours in five days. These four learning tasks in this course take three hours.

Teaching Time and Learning Time

If one sees teaching as telling, then time is not an issue. It takes much less time to tell than it does to enable people to learn cognitive content or psychomotor skills.

Learning time involves all that we have been sharing in this book: engagement of learners, physical activity, reinforcement of content, and application of new skills.

Learning time is significantly greater than teaching time. When my brilliant professor of literature at Fordham University offered his weekly lecture and finished in exactly three hours, on the dot, he was teaching. He was not, I believe, thinking about or designing for learning in that large lecture room. In that educational paradigm, his time with us was for his teaching. Our learning would take place later.

As we move to a learning-centered approach to education, we are compelled to think differently about time.

What are some of the basic problems educators face in terms of time? The ones named here relate to decision making about time for single learning tasks and articulating the entire time frame for a learning event.

How Do We Decide Who Decides?

Often, as in the industry example described at the beginning of the chapter, the time frame is given. We had to select the appropriate amount of content to share with those executives in a two-hour time frame. We might have negotiated with those who requested the course to increase the time frame; it would have been a good opportunity to show how the time frame determines what folks can and will learn.

Sometimes, as an adult educator you are allowed to name the time frame that works best for learning. You still must select the content (*what*), name the objectives (*what for*), and design the learning tasks. It is always a temptation to design too much *what* (content) for the *when* (time frame), even if you have the luxury of naming that time frame.

The decision on the time frame is contingent on the *who* (learners) and on the situation (*why*). More is not necessarily better. As an educator, you must be aware that the amount of content depends on the time frame. The content (*what*) must be your choice. If a particular situation demands that learners master a set amount of content, you must be free to determine the time frame needed.

What to Do When the Task Takes Longer Than Planned?

When learners are deeply engaged, they are often unwilling to leave the learning task. You may have allowed one half hour for a learning task on which they spend one hour, fully engaged and productive. What to do?

A rule of thumb is this: stay with the program. Trust your own timing. If it is time to share products from one learning task and move on to the next, do so. Learners' engagement does not wane as they move to the next, more difficult, task in the sequence.

Remember, learning takes place in the learning event. Learning does not end there. The time you are allotted is for *initial* learning to take place. Ongoing learning and transfer in any content field is up to the individual. Adult learners realize that not all their learning takes place within the event. They know from experience that they can continue learning at home, on the job, and on site.

Both you as educator and they as learners are guided by the design. Insofar as you do what you promised to do in the design, you are accountable. There are instances, of course, where you come to realize while teaching that your design was unrealistic; it really does take them one hour for the learning task to which you allotted thirty minutes. Although the rule of thumb about staying with the program holds, there are times when flexibility demands that you redesign the program, perhaps omitting one of the content items and therefore one of the learning tasks.

Do you recall the strategic-planning session I described (in Chapter Two) where I decided to stop the program while the group dealt with a difficult issue? We stayed with the program; we simply shortened it. Such flexibility is obviously a necessary aspect of this approach to learning.

How Do We Frame the Time?

We saw in the last chapter how important it is to indicate end times in setting a learning task. Read the learning task in question and then say, for instance, "We'll share your work at 10:15. I'll let you know when it's 10:10." Then at 10:10 you say something like, "We have five minutes to complete this task, before we share our findings."

This is precise and clean, much more effective than saying, "I'll give you twenty minutes for this task." The time for a learning task includes time for large-group sharing. So if your design has five hours in which to carry out ten learning tasks, each half-hour allotment includes both small-group work and large-group sharing.

What Does the Learners' Program Show About Time Frames?

It is my custom not to show times for each learning task on the program. My reason is simply that it never is true. You cannot be sure that you will spend exactly ten minutes on each part of a task. What you can offer is the whole picture ("We have three learning tasks that teach all the named content of this course. Each learning task will take one hour").

Your task as educator is to help learners learn, not to wield a stopwatch. You must be flexible with these numbers, knowing only that the full set of learning tasks will be completed within the time frame.

On your own copy of the program, you can write in the discrete time frames for each section. This works well for me. Remember, the rule of thumb is to stay with the program. However you do it, the learning tasks must take place with adequate time for each.

How Do We Give Learners the Whole Picture?

Whenever we begin a program and review the seven steps, we always lay out the overall time frame. In this case, we say, "We will complete nine learning tasks in the next six hours in order to learn this content." We call this large time framing. This gives the learners a clear picture of what they are starting. Such a concise statement makes for both accountable teaching and accountable learning.

How Can We Be Sure?

As you design the time frame for a set of learning tasks, always keep the allotment for tasks a bit under the given time. If you have three hours, design for two hours and forty-five minutes. If you have thirty hours, design for twenty-nine. You will be surprised how quickly the margin of time is used up.

Too Much What for Your When

No problem is so consistent as designing too much *what* for the *when*. How many times have you been at a training session or a course where the professor or instructor says, "We don't have enough time to do this thoroughly" or "If we only had enough time, we could do this well"? You will not hear those phrases in using this approach to learning-centered design, because here you design for the time you are given. You do it well—every time.

Learning Task 13: Setting Time for Learning Tasks

Task 13A: Consider a topic you are about to teach. Sketch two learning tasks you can use. Using the guideline (consider N, C, and T), allot a time frame to each learning task.

Task 13B: Identify one way large frame timing might help you in your teaching.

Task 13C: Consider the axiom that learning-centered teaching needs three things, and in this order: time, time, and time. Is it true? Why do you think so?

Synthesis

In this chapter, we have examined a basic guideline for effective use of time with learning tasks and responded to classic time problems in design and teaching. We have heard again the most common error committed by designers: too much *what* for the *when*. We have applied the guideline to the task of allotting time to a sample of teaching from our own life. In Chapter Nine, we examine the use of learning tasks in a set of diverse topics.

9

Checkpoint: Reviewing Concepts Through Examples

Learning Task 14

A theologian attended one of our recent introductory courses, "Learning to Listen, Learning to Teach." Johanna Vento was completing her doctoral studies in theology while working at a neighborhood community center in the Bronx. She was soon to be teaching theology to undergraduates and wanted to use this opportunity to try the learning-task approach on her hot topic: the idea of God.

Vento was quite dubious about using this approach. She had spent years and years in school listening to learned lectures on theology and philosophy. She and her design partner were courageous, however, and determined at least to try. I was sent out to scour the neighborhood bookstores for a copy of the writings of the European theologian Ludwig Feuerbach. Vento's dissertation is a study of this nineteenth-century theologian. She and her partner had forty minutes to share with us the essence of his teaching, by way of a design using learning tasks.

The Wizard of Oz Has Something to Teach

Feuerbach inspired L. Frank Baum, the author of *The Wizard of Oz*. The novel aside, the classic film is not often seen as the theological opus it is. We all remember the scene where the little man behind the curtain is found out by the frightened foursome as Dorothy's dog pulls aside the heavy drape to reveal his machines and machinations.

Feuerbach suggested in his theological writings that human beings have created a god in their own image, a monster busy at incredible, sadistic machinations. He suggested that God wants only to be known as friend, father, and ally—not master or monster.

Vento and her partner used a video clip of that scene from the "Wizard of Oz" and set for us learners the task of unraveling it in light of theological concepts, which she had summarized for us in a short lecture and handout. Her task, as I recall it, was "Having read this handout, and seen this video clip, in pairs name ways God has seemed like this to you in your life. . . . Then, share your impressions of this theologian's view of God as friend, father, and ally. We'll hear a sample."

I told the team afterwards that it was the first time in my history of leading this course that I wept during a practice teaching session. We were all moved, inspired, and exhausted by the small-group interaction.

I tried to imagine how her lesson might have been if she had not used a learning task. She could give us a brilliant lecture on the life and work of that theologian (though I doubt I would remember it today). By way of her design and the learning tasks she and her partner set and led, Vento brought directly to us the challenge of Feuerbach: Where do we get our idea of God? I find myself wondering if any theologian could hope to do more.

Here are some further examples of learning tasks to teach quite diverse sets of KSAs. I propose that an *attitude* is never directly taught through a learning task. Attitudes are caught, not taught. Attitudes are developed by reflection on new habits of acting. Spend a week showing respect to colleagues, and you will be en route to a deeper attitude of respect.

EXAMPLE 1: WINE APPRECIATION

Achievement-based objectives: Learners will examine a wine label to determine the percentage of alcohol, geographic source of wine, year of production, importer or distributor, and other notes offered. They will compare wines by noting the color; and by swirling, smelling (its "nose"), tasting, and savoring.

Text: *Windows on the World Complete Wine Course*, by Kevin Zraly (New York: Sterling, 1995), pp. 14–17.

WINE LEARNING TASK 1
(WINE APPRECIATION 101)

Task 1A: Everyone has a bottle of wine in hand. Let's work with the label. In pairs, tell your partner what you read on your label. Compare the percentage of alcohol, geographic source of wine, year of production, importer or distributor, and other notes offered. We'll hear a sample of your observations.

Task 1B: In new pairs, pour a glass from your bottle. Note the color of your wine. Swirl it in the glass to oxygenate it. Sniff the wine for the "nose" or aroma. Tell your partner what you would call it. Then taste the wine by moving a small mouthful slowly over all the taste buds in your mouth. Describe what you associate with the taste. Finally, savor the wine by thinking about the taste and sharing your thoughts. We'll hear a sampling of impressions.

Imagine the delicious dialogue in that room! We are assuming that all participants have read the pages from Zraly's book (and more than those pages) and that each has indeed come with a bottle of wine and a corkscrew, as directed.

If you have been to a course on wines recently, you know this is not what usually happens. Instead, a monologue by the wine expert usually precedes a very controlled wine tasting. I personally would love to enjoy the rich dialogue and good wine of this learning task.

EXAMPLE TWO: BUDDHISM 101

Achievement-based objectives: by the end of this session, everyone will name the founder of Buddhism (Siddhartha Gautama) and review the life of the Buddha; examine the four noble truths and identify the elements in the noble eightfold path.

Text: "Encarta 97" (Microsoft encyclopedia software)

BUDDHISM LEARNING TASK 1
(THE FOUNDER OF BUDDHISM)

Task 1A: Read this short description of the life of the Buddha. Circle what strikes you as vital. Share what you have circled in pairs. We'll hear a sample of comments.

Buddhism: a major world religion, founded in northeastern India and based on the teachings of Siddhartha Gautama, who is known as the Buddha, or Enlightened One.

Originating as a monastic movement within the dominant Brahman tradition of the day, Buddhism quickly developed in a distinctive direction. The Buddha not only rejected significant aspects of Hindu philosophy but also challenged the authority of the priesthood, denied the validity of the Vedic scriptures, and rejected the sacrificial cult based on them. Moreover, he opened his movement to members of all castes, denying that a person's spiritual worth is a matter of birth.

No complete biography of the Buddha was compiled until centuries after his death; only fragmentary accounts of his life are found in the earliest sources. Western scholars, however, generally agree on 563 B.C. as the year of his birth.

Siddhartha Gautama, the Buddha, was born in Kapila-vastu, near the present Indian-Nepal border, the son of the ruler of a petty kingdom. According to legend, at his birth sages recognized in him the marks of a great man with the potential to become either a sage or the ruler of an empire. The young prince was raised in sheltered luxury, until at the age of twenty-nine he realized how empty his life to this point had been. Renouncing earthly attachments, he embarked on a quest for peace and enlightenment, seeking release from the cycle of rebirths. For the next few years he practiced Yoga and adopted a life of radical asceticism.

Eventually he gave up this approach as fruitless and instead adopted a middle path between the life of indulgence and that of self-denial. Sitting under a bo tree, he meditated, rising through a series of higher states of consciousness until he attained the enlightenment for which he had been searching. Once having known this ultimate religious truth, the Buddha underwent a period of intense inner struggle. He began to preach, wandering from place to place, gathering a body of disciples, and organizing them into a monastic community known as the *sangha*. In this way he spent the rest of his life.

The Buddha was an oral teacher; he left no written body of thought. His beliefs were codified by later followers.

BUDDHISM LEARNING TASK 2
(THE FOUR NOBLE TRUTHS)

Task 2A: Read this summary of the four noble truths. In pairs, name the one that seems to speak most clearly to you. We'll hear a sample of your selections.

Task 2B: Examine this list of the four noble truths and the eightfold path. In new pairs, name the one that seems most challenging to you, and tell your partner why.

At the core of the Buddha's enlightenment was the realization of the Four Noble Truths: (1) Life is suffering. This is more than a mere recognition of the presence of suffering in existence. It is a statement that, in its very nature, human existence is essentially painful from the moment of birth to the moment of death. Even death brings no relief, for the Buddha accepted the Hindu idea of life as cyclical, with death leading to further rebirth. (2) All suffering is caused by ignorance of the nature of reality and the craving, attachment, and grasping that result from such ignorance. (3) Suffering can be ended by overcoming ignorance and attachment. (4) The path to the suppression of suffering is the Noble Eightfold Path, which consists of right views, right intention, right speech, right action, right livelihood, right effort, right mindedness, and right contemplation. These eight are usually divided into three categories that form the cornerstone of Buddhist faith: morality, wisdom, and *samadhi*, or concentration.

Notice how the learning task invites critical thinking and self-selection of concepts. This is the practice of autonomy. Without it, learning can be simple parroting of the teacher's perspective. This constructivist perspective implies that the learner must construct his or her own meaning from the available data. A learning task such as this one on Buddhism insists on that construction of meaning.

Note also the use of readings along with the input task ("Read and circle what strikes you. Share what you circled"). What would you design as an implementation or integration task for this topic?

EXAMPLE 3: MUSIC THEORY 101

Achievement-based objectives: by the end of this session all will have

- Defined an interval
- Distinguished between harmonic and melodic intervals
- Practiced designing and playing harmonic and melodic intervals

MUSIC LEARNING TASK 1 (INTERVALS)

Task 1A: Read this short excerpt.

INTERVALS An interval is the distance between two pitches. When the two pitches are aligned vertically, the interval is called a harmonic interval; when the pitches are found in succession, they are called melodic intervals. Measure intervals by the letter names they encompass: C to E is a third (C-D-E); C to G, which can also be written C–G, is a fifth (C-D-E-F-G). Accidentals do not affect numerical measurement.

Task 1B: On the piano, play any third harmonic interval. Play the same third as a melodic interval. Play a fifth melodic interval. Now play that fifth as a harmonic interval.

Task 1C: Play any octave as a harmonic interval; then as a melodic interval.

Task 1D: Play any whole step as a harmonic interval, e.g., C–D. Play that same whole step as a melodic interval.

Task 1E: Play any half step as a harmonic interval, e.g., E–F or B–C. Now play it as a melodic interval.

Task 1F: Describe the difference you see between a harmonic interval and a melodic interval.

This example shows the use of careful sequence and reinforcement. In this learning task, the learning takes place in the very task, which involves input and implementation. Psychomotor activity and practice corroborates the cognitive; the concept of interval is not only heard but also made by the learner. The final section, task 1F, invites the learner to describe his or her experience and define the two types of interval. Later, at home or at their own instruments, adult learners can transfer this learning, which first took place as they did the learning task.

These three examples—indeed, all the examples throughout this book—are designed to show that using learning tasks takes both competence in the particular content discipline on the part of the adult educator, and adequate time devoted to the process. Such is the price of accountability.

These three simple learning tasks show how you can teach diverse topics using learning tasks. The example from music shows the use of sequence and reinforcement, as well as psychomotor activity. The example from Buddhism shows how readings can be reflected upon and then applied to the learner's own life. The example from wine appreciation shows the use of physical objects (bottles of wine) and the learning potential of psychomotor activities along with cognitive material. Wine tasting has its own innate affective potential!

The example from music theory shows how vital it is to take small, well-sequenced steps in learning. Notice how each part of that learning task built on the previous part. The subtleties of designing learning tasks for your own content will keep you engaged as a teacher for the rest of your days. Let's try it now, on your own content.

Learning Task 14: Designing for Your Own Content

You know the process. Respond to the seven steps of planning:

1. *Who*: the learners (how many?).

2. *Why*: the situation that calls for this teaching and learning event. They need. . . .

3. *When*: the time frame. Be careful about having too much *what* for your *when*.

4. *Where*: the site for the work. You need an arrangement that allows learners to work together.

5. *What* (content).

6. *What for* (achievement-based objectives). What learners will do with the content in order to learn it.

7. *How* (learning tasks).

Notice that learning tasks deal specifically with each piece of content you name. Some of these are cognitive (ideas), some psychomotor (skills), and others, affective (attitudes). We do not usually teach attitudes directly. Attitudes are caught, not taught. They result from repeated behavior and from reflection on that behavior.

Synthesis

In this chapter, we have seen three diverse examples of learning tasks designed for adults. You can see that there is no content you need to teach that cannot become part of a learning task. This means we must risk changing established ways of teaching, which takes courage. Our challenge is to let go of telling, and move by design to creative learning tasks. When they finish doing such tasks, learners will say, "Look what we did—ourselves!" In Chapter Ten, we look further at designing appropriate learning tasks for all kinds of people.

10

Matching Tasks to the Group: One Size Does Not Fit All

Learning Task 15

My colleague at Hospice of the Carolinas and I had worked for months to get the attention of the Hospice Nurses Organization of the Southeast. We wanted to share with them our research on adult learning, and give them a chance to practice the skills taught in *Learning to Listen, Learning to Teach* and *Training Through Dialogue*. The nurses in this organization teach hospice staff, patients, families, medical colleagues, and community groups. They are adult educators of the first order.

Finally, it happened. We had a one-day workshop with twenty-five leaders of the organization. We worked hard on the design—but ultimately we couldn't have been more wrong. We decided these folks needed solid theory behind a dialogue approach to adult education. We used the excellent summary of Kurt Lewin's theory from Johnson and Johnson (1991), designing a learning task that invited reflection and creative application of his twelve principles.

The design was a failure! We soon realized that we had set the wrong learning task for these men and women, all of whom were relentless, active, creative nurses. They needed to be doing something—redesign their present courses, name their problems in training, work together on their real cases.

The people who learned the most that day were not, sadly, the generous hospice nurses, but the mistaken pair of educators who designed and led the workshop. As my colleague said, "We will always remember to carefully read the group before deciding the learning task."

Personality types (Jung, 1971) have been made accessible by Myers and Briggs (Briggs Myers, 1980). Today there is also growing concern about and attention to personal learning styles. We cannot aim a learning task directly at a particular type or a specific learning style. We can, however, consider these factors in our choice of learning tasks for a particular group. Type and learning style inform the choice of learning tasks. However, they do not form the learning tasks.

If, in the hospice example, we had considered our *who* in terms of their likely average type and learning style, we might have avoided the confusion and discomfort they expressed over the reflective, largely cognitive learning task we set them.

The principle here is a simple one: when naming your *who* in the seven steps of planning, consider how type and learning styles might prevail among them. This is not to say that we restrict the kinds of learning task we offer. All types and people of all learning styles need to be challenged beyond their natural inclinations and comfort zone. However, as responsible designers, we keep type and style in mind.

Learning Task 15: Make a Match

Task 15A: Consider these groups of learners. Name the kinds of learning task you would avoid with each group.

Group one: busy executives. These are well-dressed, busy executives come together to do a one-day, five-hour workshop on Peter Senge's *The Fifth Discipline: The Art and Practice of the Learning Organization* (1990). Of the fifty participants, thirty-five are male; over half of them are white-haired seniors; all are distracted by their cell phones and palmtop computers.

Group two: homemakers. These women are determined to learn how to use a computer. There are thirty of them in the group, and more than twenty are senior citizens. Few of them have any business experience, and none of them has any experience in the world of computers.

Group three: members of the National Rifle Association. This group of forty churchgoers are card-carrying members of the NRA. They have accepted the invitation of a coalition of churches to a one-day workshop on violence in the home.

Group four: youths. These boys and girls, aged sixteen to twenty, are about to enter or are already in college. They have signed up for a course on small-business management and investing. They want to design their own personal portfolio of investments and also learn the first steps in setting up their own business.

Learning task 15B: Having considered what types of learning task to avoid, now design and describe *one* appropriate learning task for any one of these groups. How does your consideration of type and learning style inform your choice of both tasks to avoid and tasks to include?

Other Considerations

Besides type and learning style, other issues to consider when designing learning tasks are language, culture, and concept.

Language and Culture

Lincolnton, North Carolina, is a small town south of Raleigh. Cotton mills once proliferated here. In the early 1990s, a mill was closed and the workers called the Center for Community Self-Help for collaboration in designing a response to the sudden closure. Martin Eakes, the young lawyer who directs the center, invited me to join him in the meeting, since he expected he would need to design a program of training for all the closed-out workers.

Eakes comes from Greensboro, North Carolina, by way of Princeton, Yale, and southern Africa. At Yale law school, whenever he was chided by colleagues "What's a southern boy like you doing here?" he would reply, "I couldn't get into UNC Law." His good humor and deep knowledge of southern culture endeared him to the Lincolnton workers, who spoke to him in a North Carolina dialect I could hardly comprehend. After listening to them chat for a while, I called him aside and told him I felt it best if I played the silent partner. I said, "They'll never understand me, nor I them!"

He smiled. "Just stand by, Jane, and keep observing, so we know how to design a good program for these folks." I did just that and spent the evening with the community, smiling a lot, but never opening my mouth to say a word. Silence can be golden.

One Size Does Not Fit All

In these days of e-commerce, global marketing, and virtual everything, it is easy to mistake the least common denominator for a decisive factor. Packaged educational products assume homogeneity among learners that we know does not exist. But in our approach to education as dialogue, we must be aware of the cultural, linguistic, typological, and epistemological differences among the learners.

The discussion at the end of Chapter Seven about three levels of questions (personal, categorical, and epistemological) is another tool for ensuring that your design is appropriate for your learners.

Recently, I heard of a presentation made by a state educator to a large group of adult basic education instructors at their annual staff-development workshop. The friend who told me this story is a supervisor of these hard-working teachers. The bureaucrat-presenter came unprepared to the session, admitting that the speech he would give them had been prepared for a conference of university administrators he attended in New Orleans the week before. I hope you are enraged, good reader. I was.

Culture as a Type

Attention to the culture of a set of learners is a form of respect. Such attention can elicit the data needed to design appropriate learning tasks. When the United Nations physician described in Chapter Six rolled up his sleeves to show his engagement with the learning task, he showed us that we had, in fact, designed to accommodate his culture. All that we ask is attention to the cultural mores of your learners. This attention can be demonstrated, and the data gathered, through a simple learning needs assessment.

When I teach at the School of Public Health of the University of North Carolina at Chapel Hill, I use a five-minute telephone call to each student to establish baseline data. This often shocks graduate students, who are incredulous that their professor wants to chat with them about their background.

I always have a potluck supper at my home as well, prior to beginning the course. There I meet graduate students, their spouses and children, their friends and partners. There I discover that this young man has just come back from China, where he served as a medical assistant; and this woman is a physician from Chile with long experience in cardiology. I discover, in this leisurely fashion, the culture of the group.

This discovery informs the kinds of learning task I can set. In a way, the students shape the parameters of their own learning by their experience and purpose. Another physician from Latin America who took this course told me, "That experience with you pushed me so hard that I was able to design the community health-education project I had dreamed about." This kind of transfer and ultimate impact on him and his corps of medical doctors could not have occurred without respect for his culture (and more broadly the cultures of the group of graduate students).

Culture is not sacrosanct. The first president of Guinea Bissau, Amilcar Cabral (1979), spoke wisely of the possibility of culture being insidious. He warned against uncritical worship of one's culture. When culture destroys life, prevents learning, or excludes anyone, it is dangerous. Respect for and attention to culture as type does not always mean accommodation to prevailing cultural norms.

Working to design a program for a major industry here in the Research Triangle, I soon became aware that decisions were being made to accommodate a lone, dominating manager—who was not even going to be present at the course. I had to reveal the problem I saw in this situation to those who employed me; I knew I had no choice. They were shocked by this kind of candor, but finally they agreed that I could not work with them under these circumstances— which were not going to change.

When culture works against learning, we must at least voice our perception, and then choose how involved we can be. This learning-centered approach has the delightful quality of uncovering domination and oppressive purposes. A dominating manager quickly discovers that you are the wrong educator to strengthen his control over the workers or staff. At times, exit is eminent success. My exit from any number of such situations was perhaps the best educating I could do.

Our Subjective Stamp of Approval

As we decide what types and learning styles seem to prevail, we are strengthened by the knowledge of the power of our own type and learning style. On the Myers-Briggs Type Indicator scale (MBTI), I am an extravert, intuitive, feeling, perceiving type (ENFP); I learn most quickly and effectively if I am engaged physically and visually. Now, that's the kind of learner I like! If I were not conscious of what this chapter is trying to teach about type, all of my learning tasks would look like me.

Examine your designs for your own type and learning style, and also for your own culture. We can strive to be conscious of how personal and ethnocentric our designs are, and once conscious, we can make decisions based on our responses to the seven steps of planning. The learning tasks may never satisfy and be congruent with all the cultures and types present, but your conscious decision cannot help but show learners how much you respect them.

Synthesis

In this chapter, we have shown how learning tasks can be informed by awareness of type, learning style, and cultural preferences. We have examined how far such information can affect our decisions. We have also acknowledged the need for creativity and perseverance in designing and using learning needs-assessment processes, and we have noted the general probability of designers creating the kinds of learning task that match their own type and style and culture. In Chapter Eleven, we examine how learning tasks can inform the design and function of distance-learning and Internet courses.

11

Tasks for Distance Learning and the Internet

Learning Tasks 16 and 17

My friend Peter Smith is an ardent historian. He has read more about the origins of the United States and the American democratic system than anyone I know. He is a carpenter, not an academic. When he heard of graduate courses in American history being offered on the Internet by major universities, he was overjoyed. He was prepared to learn.

Smith enrolled, paid his fees, and set to work. Imagine his disappointment when what he got for his efforts was essentially a textbook, broken into chapters, with "exercises" set out on the individual chapters, and a series of closed quiz questions that demanded nothing more than rote memory for response.

This young carpenter was prepared to grapple with ideas, to argue with peers, to sit at the feet of an equally ardent professor and do set learning tasks in order to expand his knowledge and corroborate his passion for the complexities of the democratic process.

He discovered, unfortunately, that what Freire called the "banking system of education" was now available electronically to a worldwide audience. "That," said Smith, "is not progress."

Paloff and Pratt (1999) agree with him: "Without the purposeful formation of an online learning community in distance learning, we are doing nothing new and different. . . . The development of a learning community in the distance education process involves developing new approaches to education and new skills in its delivery" (p. 161).

Learning Task 16: Learning Tasks Can Make the Difference

Examine this small section of the online course Smith was taking. The section begins with one of the objectives of the chapter in the "History of the Internet" course, framed first as an outcomes-based objective. Examine the simple changes suggested relating content to objectives and then to learning tasks, and tell how you can use this approach when you design Internet or distance-education courses.

TASK 1 (REFRAME THE OBJECTIVES)

In this chapter, you will

- Describe the constitutional provisions related to the presidency

  To ensure a learning-centered approach, and to lead directly into appropriate and engaging learning tasks, we can name the specific sample content, then reframe the objective as an achievement-based objective, and design an appropriate learning task.

- Outcomes-based objective: you will be able to name the constitutional source of the office of the president.

  To reframe this outcomes-based objective, we define *what*, *what for*, and *how*:

- *What* (content): constitutional provisions related to the presidency.

- *What for* (achievement-based objective): by the end of this session, everyone will have defined the constitutional provisions for the presidency and compared the Articles of Confederation and the Constitution of 1786.

- *How* (learning task and the following materials).

HISTORY LEARNING TASK 1 (THE CONSTITUTIONAL SOURCE OF THE OFFICE)

Read pages 315–322 of the textbook on the constitutional source of the presidency. Go on the net to www.gov.libraryof-congress. Find and read the Articles of Confederation and the Constitution of 1789. What are the differences you perceive in the two documents as they describe the office of the president? Share your response with colleagues, and then send it via e-mail to your professor, marked Learning Task 1.

As you can see, it is not difficult to make the changes that transform the given chapter objectives into achievement-based objectives that relate directly to content. These changes do, however, manifest the new approach to learning developed by Paloff and Pratt, and also a radical change in the attitude of the professor. Setting achievement-based objectives and designing learning tasks to accompany data and information is nothing less than radical. Doing so shows that the professor is open to critical thinking on the part of the learner, willing to enter into a healthy argument, and knowledgeable about how human beings learn.

The changes in format as we reframe a course toward accountable, engaged learning are not that difficult. They do demand design work on the part of a professor, and a deep sense of what a learning-centered approach looks like. As one designs learning tasks, it is inevitable that the sequence of the input and the congruence between material and objectives be examined and amended. You may find that you have omitted a learning task on vital content.

Notice that each learning task has a title that parallels the content (*what*) and achievement-based objective (*what for*) in the course design. The design of learning tasks makes the material, the learners, and also the professor accountable. As professors design virtual courses this way, they can learn how to sharpen the focus of traditional classroom courses. My colleague in South Africa, Sarah Gravett, says: "Everything hinges on the learning task. I do not give assignments any more. I design, and students complete, learning tasks. The students are the subjects of the learning operation."

Learning tasks are a natural format for Internet courses. They can result in a complete portfolio of materials developed by a student. This portfolio, rather than a grade on a test, can be clear and explicit evidence of learning. The Internet offers an opportunity for a community of learners to review one another's learning tasks.

The Ontological Advantage

There are technical issues in designing a distance-learning course on the Internet that we do not address here. Remember Oliver's distinction (1989) between technical and ontological learning? As Paloff and Pratt explain, "The learning process in the electronic classroom is an active one. The ability to think before responding and to comment whenever the student wishes helps to create a level of participation and engagement that goes much deeper" (1999, p. 6).

Careful design of Internet courses can provide both technical and ontological knowing. This is our chance as educators to learn to listen not only to our adult students but also to the world they live in. When we use a demanding learning-centered approach, design accountable learning tasks, and have adult students create autonomous and creditable portfolios of evidence of their personal learning, we are in dialogue. The Internet offers us a chance to listen to learners and to develop teamwork and collaborative skills among learners as they share their research and discoveries.

When I hear someone speak of grading on a curve, I offer a challenge: "The only curve we are involved with is the curve of this global sphere." Imagine the excitement of learners in Iran and Tanzania and Indonesia sharing perceptions of the origins of the office of the presidency in the United States of America, with one another and with an educator who is teaching and learning at the same time.

As Paloff and Pratt argue, we need a new approach to learning and teaching for this new electronic classroom. How adroitly the Internet can reveal the moment of death of the professor. All we need to do is celebrate this death and the emerging community life that means learning is occurring naturally and spontaneously all over the globe.

Distance Learning

Much of what we see in distance-learning courses shows the same problems described in Internet courses: learners get a textbook and exercises; and they rarely get sequenced, considered learning tasks.

Learning Task 17: Text-Based Courses for Distance Learning

Task 17A: Describe what you see as the difference in the usual text-based course for distance learning and one using this learning-centered approach with learning tasks.

Task 17B: In your perception, how does a learning task differ from the usual "exercises" that follow assigned reading in a distance-learning course?

In Appendix B, we offer excerpts from a learning-centered distance-learning course that is being used in South Africa through the Faculty of Education at Rand Afrikaans University. The course has been designed with the seven steps of planning. The government of South Africa requires all distance-learning courses to have outcomes-based objectives. In this example, these objectives are shown and then translated into more specific achievement-based objectives, content pieces, and learning tasks. This course is not at present an Internet offering; however, since the patterns of design for this and Internet courses are similar, it is relatively simple to transfer it from text to an electronic format.

Synthesis

In this chapter, we have shown how simple the changes are that can move distance-learning and Internet courses into a learning-centered pattern, with achievement-based objectives and learning tasks. We have pointed to Appendix B for examples of Internet and distance-learning courses using this approach. In Chapter Twelve, we read a synthesis of this book in the form of twenty good reasons for using learning tasks and twenty corollary principles to guide their design.

12

Using Learning Tasks: Twenty Reasons and Twenty Principles

Learning Tasks 18 and 19

Ellen Turgasen was working as a hospice nurse. She was very clear that her job was not only to control pain and bind wounds but also to educate patients and their families about health, disease, and the resources hospice offered them.

Turgasen worked in rural North Carolina. The families and patients she met loved her and reveled in her attention and professional competence, at a time in their lives when such attention and competence were badly needed.

She is a JUBILEE Fellow, having studied this approach to adult learning for years. She constantly reports delightful ways she incorporates the principles and practices of adult learning into her hospice work.

One day, she went to a new patient. Sam Smith was an old fellow who lived with his elderly wife in a trailer. He was dying from a particularly virulent cancer. On her first visit, Turgasen laid out on their coffee table a set of bright, large-print cards. Each card had one of the hospice services marked on it: financial advising, counseling, medical services prescribed by doctor, chaplain services, Meals on Wheels, prescription buying service.

Ellen set for them a learning task: "Mr. Smith, these are the services hospice has to offer. I will leave these cards with you so you can consider them. Right now, tell me which of these services you and your wife might want."

He hesitated, and then a large, toothless smile spread over his leathery face: "We'll take a little bit of everything."

Designing learning tasks is difficult work. Using the seven steps of planning is a discipline not easily achieved or sustained. We all face the constant temptation to "teach"—to tell the learners what they need to know, or do, or feel. There must be a very good reason for taking the time and energy involved in designing a cogent learning-centered session in your context. In this final chapter, I propose twenty such reasons (and relate an important principle to each), which serve as a synthesis of all that is offered in this book.

Learning Task 18: Twenty Good Reasons and Twenty Principles

Task 18A: Read these twenty good reasons for using learning tasks and at the end of each reason a congruent principle. Circle those that make the most sense in your context.

Reason One: Immediate Learning

Learning occurs immediately if you use a learning task. You know now that a learning task implements an achievement-based objective, which in turn describes what learners do with the content they are learning. A learning task, we defined earlier, is an open question put to a group or individual having all the resources needed for a response. The open question demands creativity and construction, building upon previous knowledge using the resources offered.

As teachers, we cannot control the level of learning of any individual because we cannot control that previous knowledge or the genetic and social make-up of the individual. We can control the learning environment: safety in the small groups, sequence of learning tasks, aesthetics of the physical site, sufficient time for completing the learning task, and so on.

When an individual in a safe and supportive small group completes a specific learning task to implement a specific objective that teaches a relevant piece of content, the person learns the content in the course.

As we saw previously, learning is what occurs in the course, transfer is what occurs later when the learning is put to use, and impact is the perceived difference in the organization as a result of such learning and transfer. Learning tasks ensure that the learning does take place within the course or session.

In other patterns of teaching, learning is expected to take place outside the classroom, as the students work out exercises on what they were taught. Then they are tested to see if their exercises are done correctly, and to see how much of what was taught is learned. Learning tasks ensure immediate learning.

Therefore, we can set out this first principle: *Learning tasks, not teaching tasks, make for effective learning-centered education.*

Reason Two: Telling Is Not Teaching

Learning tasks stop us from merely telling. Teaching as telling has long been suspect. Who among us has not struggled with some addiction and been angered by the pious injunction of others to "Just say no!"? How many of us have stared at test responses from students and complained, "But I told them that in September!"?

Telling is not teaching. Socrates knew that, Jesus knew that, and the Buddha lived that wisdom. Why then do we resort to telling? My thesis is that we have not had a viable, accessible alternative.

One alternative is the learning task. In a well-designed learning task that implements a sound achievement-based objective to teach relevant content, the material we would otherwise "tell" is examined, critiqued, reconstructed, recreated, applied, and tested. Compare this to telling, where the content is merely heard.

Here is our second principle: *The more teaching (telling) there is, the less learning there is.*

Reason Three: Engagement

Engagement is ensured with learning tasks. Throughout the twentieth century, research moved educators to recognize what we knew all along: without engagement there is no learning. Shakespeare wrote of the child "slouching unwillingly to school"–surely not to be engaged in a relevant learning project!

Learning tasks in this approach demand engagement—and are designed for it. Remember: a learning task is for the learner. It is easy to slip back into designing teaching tasks, stating in our lesson plans what the teacher will do. Such teaching tasks do not demand the kind of engagement needed for effective learning.

We design learning tasks to be accomplished in pairs, in small groups of four to six people, or individually. In any case, it is the learners who meet the content head on to complete a learning task.

The French have a phrase for it: *On peut s'engager* ("You can get involved in this!"). Do you remember the 1989 film *Dead Poets Society*, starring Robin Williams? Do you recall the high level of engagement of those boys as they crept out of their dorms in the middle of the night to recite poetry to one another?

In a series of interviews with Bill Moyers on public television, Joseph Campbell (1991) spoke of the flush he perceived in the face of a young woman student he was counseling when, in conversation, he struck a theme that was meaningful to her. Her engagement had a clear physical indicator.

The engagement provoked by well-designed learning tasks is reason enough to go to the trouble of using the seven steps of planning and preparing a learning-centered design.

This third principle stands: *Without the engagement of the learners, there is no lasting learning.*

Reason Four: Inviting Critical Thinking

Learning tasks invite critical thinking. We know from our experience as learners and teachers that we do not learn anything until we contest it, question the research base, argue that it is possible that an alternative is true.

A great example of how critical thinking works in learning is my own experience with the study of St. Matthew's gospel at a graduate course in a small university in Minnesota. What the professor was offering us in terms of an interpretation of that gospel was so radical, so far from what we had learned in school from the good nuns, that I had a huge struggle with him and with his position. I wanted to see his sources, to hear why he took this position, to examine other, older interpretations.

In this struggle (which the professor deeply enjoyed), I recreated his theories. This was cognitive construction of the first order. What finally emerged was cut to fit my cloth.

When I completed that course, I felt I understood his teaching and the thematic links between Jesus and Moses that he showed in this most Jewish of all gospels. I had put his content to the test, approaching it as Jacob did the angel, wrestling with it.

This is the quality of learning that a learning task can invite. So, a fourth principle is: *When you contest it, you are probably learning it well*.

Reason Five: Critical Feeling

Learning tasks invite the teacher to be concerned about critical feeling. Just as we try to teach for critical thinking by inviting reflection and response to data, so can we teach for critical feeling.

Teaching for critical feeling involves concern for the emotional context of the learners. It demands a level of consciousness in the teacher or course designer such that the material being taught is offered with respect to the life and context of the learners.

In her response to the Literacy Volunteers of America training course, one woman acknowledged Malcolm Knowles's classic figures on retention by saying, "I agree we remember 20 percent of what we hear, 40 percent of what we hear and see, and 80 percent of what we do. I also know I remember 100 percent of what I feel."

Principle five: *Affective engagement is also an imperative*.

Reason Six: Comprehensive Work

A learning task ensures comprehensive work with all content. We have seen how using the seven steps of planning focuses and integrates learning. The *how* learning tasks and materials implement the *what for* (achievement-based objectives), which in turn show what learners do with the *what*—the content.

For many years, I was concerned that teaching teams in our introductory course, "Learning to Listen, Learning to Teach," rarely used film clips in their teaching practice. Now, one of our achievement-based objectives is that learners will examine a video clip and identify ways to use it effectively.

In leading the course, Joye Norris noticed that we had no learning task for the latter part of that objective. We did in fact examine a video clip, but we did it as a synthesis task for the elements of adult learning, not for the purposes indicated in the objective.

Once we put in a new learning task inviting learners to name the advantages of using a video clip and to practice selecting and using one, the number of teams using video clips in their teaching designs rose dramatically.

Without the design pattern of *what*, *what for*, and *how*, we can remain ignorant of the gaps in our designs. Such gaps prevent accountable teaching and learning. The planning steps show us how the content, objectives, and learning tasks are linked.

The synthesis principle here is: *Content, objectives, and learning tasks are intrinsically linked.*

Reason Seven: Ensuring Completion

Learning tasks also ensure completion of all achievement-based objectives. The charm of achievement-based objectives is that they make it certain all content is thoroughly taught. However, it is possible to design a set of achievement-based objectives but fail to have an equal set of learning tasks implementing those objectives.

Again, the parallel arrangement of content, objectives. and learning tasks protects us against empty promises. The set of learning tasks forces us to be accountable.

The seventh principle: *Every objective has a set of learning tasks*.

Reason Eight: Indications of Learning

Products of learning tasks offer substantive indicators of learning. We saw in Chapter Eight how the best verbs for learning tasks are those that produce. If learners who have in fact designed an addition to their homes to show their grasp of a set of mathematical concepts and processes, they know they know! The math can be checked and corrected, the draft designs realigned as needed, and the visions of their new sunrooms celebrated through the tangible, substantive products of effective learning tasks.

When we refer to learning tasks and materials as the *how* in the seven steps of planning, we mean not only content pieces such as readings and lecture notes but also the materials learners can use to produce the appropriate product.

Active learning means productive learning. When adult educators leave the introductory course we have mentioned, they carry away two designs that they created using all the content they learned through the week. They get a full report of the course, with their own design and those of all their colleagues. This is a necessary product of their learning.

Here, then, is principle eight: *The better the product, the better the learning*.

Reason Nine: Solid Evaluation

Evaluation can be focused and accurate if learning tasks are set. Earlier in this text we examined the three aspects of evaluation offered in *How Do They Know They Know* (Vella, Berardinelli, and Burrow, 1998). As you will recall, they are learning, transfer, and impact. During a course or session we can usually only evaluate learning.

Since using the seven steps of planning and learning tasks involves learners' doing something with what they are learning, there are accurate and focused data available to learners and teachers alike as to the quality of the learning.

If it is a matter of a skill, one can see learners perform it then and there, as a result of a learning task. If it is an idea, one can examine the product demanded by the learning task in relation to the idea: a construct, an essay, a critique, a comparison, a map, a time line, a collage. If it is an attitude, one can feel the difference. Attitudes, as we have said, are more caught than taught. They take time to develop and to test. Learning tasks do not often deal directly with attitudes.

The ninth principle: *If we can see, hear, touch, taste, and smell the learning, we can evaluate it specifically and accurately.*

Reason Ten: Group Dialogue

The structure of learning tasks invites intragroup dialogue. Every aspect of our modern world demands teamwork. When men and women are in a learning situation, working together on learning tasks, they are practicing teamwork.

A good learning task is set for collaborative action, where learners use the teacher as a resource person, not as a leader or all-knowing reference. The learning takes place as the dialogue among the learners develops.

Here we see the difference between peer telling and "expert" telling. Peer telling is a catalyst to learning whenever it is focused and deeply felt.

In this approach to learning, one of the teacher's hardest jobs is to sit down, keep quiet, pay attention, and not intrude or "help" with any learning task.

Principle number ten: *Effective learning tasks are tasks for the learners done in teams.*

Reason Eleven: Learner as Subject, Not Object

Learners are invited to be subjects of their own learning if they are engaged in learning tasks. Philosophers and literary giants of the eighteenth century recognized that the incipient industrial revolution was built on the assumption that "hands" ran machines, and "legs" ran errands. Men and women were objectified to produce goods that produced wealth. In response to this gross misconception, the philosopher Hegel emphasized that men and women are designed by nature to be subjects—decision makers—in their own lives, not to be objects to be used by others.

This approach to learning insists on learners working always as subjects (decision makers) as they complete learning tasks that are intentionally open questions. We all need this practice, more so in the year 2000 and beyond. Hegel was right.

Principle eleven: *Learners learn if they recognize themselves as subjects (decision makers) of their own learning*.

Reason Twelve: Diversity of Learning

Learning tasks can be diverse for all types of learner. As we have noted, Carl Jung's 1921 volume *Psychological Types* has been made accessible through the work of Isabel Briggs Myers and colleagues. Today there is great emphasis on consideration of learning styles as they relate to personality types.

As we design learning tasks, we know they must be comprehensive in dealing with not just the entire set of content but also the diverse types of learners.

A reflective learning task can follow an active, inductive, affective learning task. A physical learning task can be followed by a quiet reading task. No one learning task appeals to all types or all learning styles, although I have seen different people use the same learning task to fit their own type and style.

As long as we are faithful to making a learning task an implied open question put to a small group having all the resources they need to respond, then how they use those resources, how they respond, and how they work together can be their choice. Our job as designers and teachers is to diversify. Theirs is to learn, in their own way.

Thus we have principle twelve: *We need diverse learning tasks for diverse personality types and learning styles*.

Reason Thirteen: Involving All Learning Functions

Learning tasks involve cognitive, affective, and psychomotor functions. Since learning tasks are designed to teach cognitive content, physical skills, and attitudes, they involve all three functions: cognitive (or meaning making), affective (or feeling clarification), and psychomotor (or muscle function). Some learning tasks are tasks of the mind, some are of the heart, and some are of the muscles. Most good learning tasks integrate all three.

Again, one reason to use learning tasks is the potential for diversity: a thoughtful, contemplative learning task dealing with cognitive content or ideas and concepts can be followed by a skill-building, physically active learning task. As learning tasks are being completed, the affective qualities of the process can be made explicit by learning tasks within learning tasks ("Share at your table what you were feeling as you completed that project together. We'll hear a sample of your shares").

The thirteenth principle: *Three elements are essential for effective learning: ideas, actions, and feelings*.

Reason Fourteen: Sequence and Safety

The sequence of learning tasks affords safety for learners. As we design to teach any set of content and implement any set of achievement-based objectives, we can set out the learning tasks in a sequence that enhances safety: from easy to difficult, from simple to complex, from group to individual.

We can look at a series of learning tasks and see the developmental aspects within the sequence.

In Chapter Eleven, we examined the potential of this approach for distance learning and working on the Internet. Imagine how reassuring a clear sequence of learning tasks are to an isolated learner who, no doubt, has fears about his or her potential for success.

The fourteenth principle: *Presenting learning tasks in a careful, gentle sequence ensures safety and learning.*

Reason Fifteen: Inclusion

Using small groups in learning tasks allows inclusion. In my experience, small-group implementation of a learning task is an effective way of including the shy or resistant learner. Remember the UN physician who finally took off his coat and rolled up his sleeves to get involved with his peers in a meaningful learning task?

In a traditional classroom, where learning tasks are not used, individuals can be excluded from the learning process. Learning tasks completed in small groups deal with the possibility of such exclusion.

Without inclusion, a learning group is fragmented. If a learner feels excluded, he or she not only becomes restless but often also acts out. I have seen resistance coming from unexpected quarters and recognized that it was from an individual who, for some reason, felt excluded.

The issue of motivation is also addressed here. If a learner feels included in the work involved in completing a learning task, he or she is moved to collaborate. The most heated arguments and deliberations indicate a motivated group of learners who are learning.

Principle fifteen: *Inclusion is necessary for comprehensive learning.*

Reason Sixteen: Documentation

Learning tasks lead to comprehensive documentation. Completing learning tasks permits documentation of the learning. Such documentation serves as a reminder to learners, and as a tribute to the design and teaching.

If learning tasks are set out in a report, along with the products of those tasks, there can be little doubt about the learning that took place. For example, in one strategic-planning session participants not only learned the concepts involved in program management and strategic planning but also produced a strategic plan for the next year. This plan was produced by the entire group. The product is the proof of learning.

A document or report using a sequence of learning tasks shows developmental aspects of an event: from simple tasks and products to complex, from easy work to more difficult, from group tasks to individual performance and products.

Thus, principle sixteen: *With learning tasks, documentation can be clear and comprehensive.*

Reason Seventeen: Teacher Learning

In dialogue using learning tasks, the teacher can also learn. Setting an effective learning task to teach substantive content and achieve a relevant objective is inviting learning, for learners and teachers alike.

Since a learning task is an open question put to a small group having the resources they need to respond, the teacher never knows what their response will be. Their context and experience shape that response. It is always a great surprise to discover what adult learners do with what seems like prosaic content.

Is this perhaps why educators do not use learning tasks? Is there a prevailing class attitude that prevents teachers' learning from students? If so, it is a critical handicap to the evolution of education.

In Chapter Seven we examined the skills needed to lead learning tasks well. Teachers can learn only if they are willing to welcome the most unexpected responses to their open questions, and only if they recognize that every learning task is a research agenda.

Principle seventeen: *Teachers as well as learners learn when learning tasks are used.*

Reason Eighteen: Time Management

Using learning tasks makes time management more efficient. Chapter Eight dealt with the very important issue of time and learning tasks. Here, we offer a cogent reason for using learning tasks: time is readily managed if we use learning tasks.

The *when* in our seven steps of planning invites a clear and definite statement of the time frame for a learning event. We have seen how dangerous it is to plan too much *what* for the *when*.

A set of learning tasks that fits the time frame uses the time efficiently. The content is laid out thoroughly through the input learning task, and implementation and integration tasks engage learners with the content and show them how well they have learned it.

As we saw in principle two, learning tasks prevent telling, which often uses time for the advantage only of the teller. During telling, learners are passive. Passive learners learn one thing: passivity.

It has been my experience that a set of learning tasks can teach a set of content in any discipline in less time than a teaching event, where the teacher tells and then asks learners to do an exercise.

As seen in Chapter Eight, the greatest demand on our time as teachers is in preparing effective learning tasks, not in the learning itself.

Principle eighteen: *Learning tasks use time well.*

Reason Nineteen: Unlimited Content

Vast amounts of data can be efficiently dealt with in learning tasks. There is no limit to the amount of content that can be taught in a set of learning tasks. Remember the four kinds of learning tasks: inductive, input, implementation, and integration. Input tasks can involve reading pages of data, viewing a video clip, using the Internet to access current data, using an encyclopedia, listening to a lecture, and examining data charts and handouts.

Again, sequencing this content, and segmenting it, can help learners deal with it creatively through learning tasks. Part of our preparation work is organizing vast amounts of cognitive content; or complex skills into simple, sequenced learning tasks.

Principle nineteen, then, is: *No amount of content is too much for a well-sequenced set of learning tasks.*

Reason Twenty: Foundation of the Four I's

The four I's are a useful model for preparing any educational session. With the exception of the seven steps of planning, no tool has been so useful in designing a single learning session as the four I's: inductive work, input, implementation, and integration. Using this set, any teacher can design a comprehensive, respectful, accountable session.

Imagine the four I's informing a graduate course, an orientation to a new job, a staff development seminar, a staff meeting, a technical training, a political seminar, and even a forum of presidential candidates. We could *all* be learning, and learning how to learn.

Our final principle: *The sequence of the four I's forms a useful matrix for planning a single session.*

Learning task 18B (evaluating the twenty reasons): Use Table 12.1 to see a summary of reasons and principles. Circle the ones that make the most sense in your context.

One Educator's Experience

In August 1999, I was just about to leave for Johannesburg to work there when I received an e-mail from my colleague Sarah Gravett of Rand Afrikaans University. It read, in part:

> I am really looking forward to discussing learning tasks with you. As I said—I have been trying to use learning tasks for quite a while, but still find it difficult to design

TABLE 12.1 Twenty Reasons and Derived Principles.

Reason Number (See Text)	Description of Reason	Derived Principle
1	Learning can occur immediately in using learning task.	Learning tasks make for effective learning-centered education.
2	Stops "telling."	The more teaching, the less learning.
3	Engagement is ensured with learning tasks.	Without engagement of learner, there is no effective learning.
4	Learning tasks invite critical thinking.	Until we contest what we are learning, we do not learn it.
5	Learning tasks invite teacher to be concerned about critical feeling.	To achieve accountable learning, our task is to respect learners' context.
6	Learning tasks ensure comprehensive work with all content.	Every *what* (content piece) needs a set of learning tasks.
7	Learning tasks ensure completion of achievement-based objectives.	Every *what* (content piece) has a parallel set of learning tasks.
8	Products of learning tasks offer substantive indicators of learning.	Indicators of learning can be immediate and tangible.
9	Evaluation can be focused and accurate in using learning tasks.	Indicators of learning can be immediate and tangible.
10	Structure of learning tasks evokes intragroup dialogue.	Specific evaluation relates to specific content and objectives.
11	Learners are invited to be subjects of their own learning when using learning tasks.	Testing is corroboration, not proof.
12	Learning tasks can be diverse for all types of learners.	We need diverse learning tasks for diverse groups and styles.
13	Learning tasks involve cognitive, affective, and psycho-motor functions.	Learning tasks involve cognitive content (ideas, concepts), affective content, and psychomotor action.

TABLE 12.1 Twenty Reasons and Derived Principles, Cont'd.

Reason Number (See Text)	Description of Reason	Derived Principle
14	Sequence of learning tasks affords safety for learners.	Sequence is from easy to difficult, from simple to complex, and from group to individual tasks.
15	Small-group operation with learning tasks allows inclusion.	No one is excluded from learning-centered designs.
16	Learning events using learning tasks can be readily documented.	Documentation depicts learning tasks and their products.
17	In dialogue ensured by learning task, teacher can also learn.	In creative process of learning-centered design, teacher is also learner.
18	Time is readily managed and efficiently used in learning with learning tasks.	Avoiding too much *what* for the *when* is possible in setting up learning tasks.
19	Vast amounts of data can be accountably dealt with in learning task.	Substantive content is the heart of learning tasks.
20	The Four I's are useful matrix for designing any educational session using learning tasks.	Inductive work, input, implementation, and integration offer a useful sequence of learning tasks.

meaningful tasks. One thing that I have realized many times while struggling is that it is much easier to be a teacher who uses monologue! What I have also realized—you truly become a co-learner when working with learning tasks—in two ways: The design of learning tasks requires that you deeply interact with the content. You look at the learning material that you thought you knew intimately with new eyes. You sometimes start to question ideas that you took for granted. Secondly—when working with learning tasks in class you encounter student ideas and questions that you haven't fore-seen—indeed a learning experience for a teacher!

One thing that I often wonder about: I believe that one should take students' current ways of thinking and doing as the base for teaching. Thus, when addressing a new theme I will always start with a learning task that aims at eliciting these. I then believe that one should build the rest of your teaching on and around this. If one, for example, realizes that students have major misconceptions that will interfere with the new learning, I believe that one first needs to design learn-ing tasks to address this, even though this was not part of your initial plan. I thus find it very difficult to design all the learn-ing tasks related to a specific theme neatly before interacting with learners. I often change what I planned initially. I thus find planning to be a "messy process"—not as neat as your 7 steps seem to suggest [Gravett e-mail, Aug. 12, 1999].

Learning Task 19: Synthesis

Task 19A: After having read this book, what would you say to Gravett?

Task 19B: Examine the example of a distance-learning course in Appendix B, which was composed using learning tasks. In that course, where do you see the "messy process" she describes in this e-mail?

Epilogue

Designing and using learning tasks involves a change of heart as well as a new set of skills. I am deeply aware of how difficult it can be. I wish you all the best as you experiment with this learning-cen-tered approach.

Appendix A
Learning Tasks in Action:
A Workshop Model

We will be teaching these seven steps of planning for a learning-centered design during the ninety-minute workshop, so we use them here to illustrate what the workshop will do as a learning-centered design. We believe that educators must do what they are teaching, must be congruent in their actions with their own best theories. We will model that congruence in this short workshop.

The Seven Steps of Planning

1. *Who* (participants): a group of educators at the Lilly-Atlantic Conference on College and University Teaching.

2. *Why:* the Lilly Foundation holds annual conferences around the country on college and university teaching. This is a great forum to share this research on accountable teaching for sustainable learning. The participants need to know about this research, which they can use immediately in their own designing and teaching.

3. *When* (time frame): ninety minutes during the three-day conference, April 16–18, 1999.

"Transforming the Teacher and Learner Role: A Seven-Step Plan for Designing Learning-Centered Teaching," presented at the Lilly-Atlantic Conference on College and University Teaching, April 1999, Towson Maryland.

4. *Where* (site): Berkshire Conference Center on campus of University of Maryland, Towson. The room has small tables for four, so participants can engage in dialogue with one another and *do* what they are learning for the ninety minutes.

5. *What* (content: knowledge, skills, attitudes):

   The seven steps of planning

   Achievement-based objectives

   Learning tasks

   Accountability of your design (how do they know they know?)

   The third way: learning-centered (not learner-centered or teacher-centered)

6. *What for* (achievement-based objectives): by the end of this ninety minutes, all participants will have

   Defined the value of a warm-up

   Examined and used the seven steps of planning

   Practiced writing achievement-based objectives

   Prepared a set of learning tasks

   Defined accountability of design (how do they know they know?)

   Distinguished a learning-centered design from a learner-centered or teacher-centered design

7. *How* (learning tasks and materials)

Topical Program

- Learning task 1: Welcome (program review and expectations)
- Learning task 2: Warm-up (a moment of real learning)
- Learning task 3: The seven steps of planning a learning-centered design
- Learning task 4: "Not your father's Oldsmobile" (achievement-based objectives)

- Learning task 5: Whose learning is this, anyway? (learning tasks)

- Learning task 6: How do they know they know? (accountability)

- Learning task 7: The third way (learning-centered, not learner-centered or teacher-centered)

Since we have seven learning tasks to accomplish in ninety minutes, we can expect to complete each task in approximately ten to fifteen minutes. It is vital in adult learning to avoid having too much *what* for your *when*.

Learning Task 1: Program Review and Your Expectations

Task 1A: At your table, listen to the achievement-based objectives of this ninety-minute workshop.

Task 1B: At your table, name one or two expectations you have of this event. Write each on a card and call it out as you post it on our Expectations Chart.

Note that this brief welcome begins the partnership. The expectations, like any needs assessment, do not form but do inform the program. Notice that the dialogue is not only between learner and leaders, but first and foremost among learners.

Learning Task 2: Warm-up (a Moment of Real Learning)

In pairs, describe a moment of real learning in your life: a class, a study, an encounter. Identify one remarkable and memorable factor that was at work to make that learning so memorable. We'll hear all the factors.

Note that the research being done in this short workshop uses the life experience of the participants. This is a great model. Notice also that this learning task establishes the fact that a learning-centered learning event can take place.

Learning Task 3: Take Seven Giant Steps (the Seven Steps of Planning)

Task 3A: Examine the seven steps of planning, set on your table. Put the steps in the order you agree would be useful in designing an effective course or class or workshop. When you have reached agreement, go around and look at what other tables have done.

Task 3B: Examine the seven steps of planning in the design for this workshop. What are your questions?

Learning Task 4: "Not Your Father's Oldsmobile" (Achievement-Based Objectives)

Task 4A: Look at the *what for* (achievement-based objectives) in the design for this workshop. In new pairs, change those into classic outcomes-based educational objectives, for example, "will be able to. . . ."

Task 4B: At your table, name the difference you perceive between achievement-based objectives and classic educational objectives. We'll hear all.

Learning Task 5: Who's Learning Is This, Anyway? (Learning Tasks)

A learning task is a task for the learner.

Task 5A: At a new table, examine the six learning tasks in this program. To you, what is unique about them?

Task 5B: What relation do you see between the content, the achievement-based objectives, and the learning tasks?

Task 5C: How does this differ from traditional teaching and learning?

Learning Task 6: How Do They Know They Know? (Accountability)

Task 6A: In new pairs, describe one upcoming educational event you are planning where you might try to use what you have just learned of this learning-centered approach.

Task 6B: Write one achievement-based objective for that event. Share it at your table.

Task 6C ("How do they know they know? They just did it!"): In the large group, name one way you see this approach fostering accountability.

Learning Task 7: The Third Way (Learning-Centered Design for Accountable Education)

Task 7A: We designed this workshop to be learning-centered. You did what we promised you would do. Decide upon some words that might describe *learning-centered* as you understand it now. We'll write them all to create a descriptive collage.

Appendix B
Example of a Distance-Learning Course

The distance-learning course has three component sets of materials:

1. Coursebook
2. Book of readings
3. Workbook

This workbook is where you write your learning tasks.* It will ultimately be a portfolio of your knowledge about facilitating adult learning.

Unit One is on planning learning events for adult learners (the seven steps of planning).

Here are one outcome and four objectives for this unit:

Learning Outcome	*Achievement-Based Objectives*
When you have finished working through this unit you will be able to use the seven steps of planning to design learning events.	By the time you finish working through this unit, you will have: Examined a specific approach to designing adult learning (the seven steps of planning)

* You will encounter many *learning tasks* throughout this module. It will gradually become clear to you what exactly a learning task is and why we view learning tasks as a crucial part of an accountable design for facilitating adult learning. For now, a brief definition suffices. A learning task is a task for the learner; it is an open question accompanied by the resources (the new content or learning material) learners need to respond to that open question. Learning tasks are used to structure the dialogue with adult learners.

Compared this set of planning steps to others

Identified the connection between achievement-based objectives (*what for*) and learning outcomes

Designed part of a learning event using the seven steps of planning

Learning Task 1: Next Learning Event

Describe in one short paragraph the next learning event that you will be planning. (For example: "The next learning event I will be planning is a staff development workshop on time management for secretaries in a company.")

Learning Task 2: Introducing the Seven Steps of Planning

Task 2A: Examine the summary of the seven steps of planning that follows.

THE SEVEN STEPS OF PLANNING

According to Vella (1994a), seven questions need to be answered in planning a learning event:

1. *Who?* Asking this question invites a profile of the participants and the number expected. *Profile* implies that the educator needs to find out as much as possible about the participants prior to the educational event.
2. *How?* Answering the question *how* leads to the structure of the program, the learning tasks, and materials to be used.
3. *Why?* Answering this question reveals the situation that calls for the educational event. A good way to respond to this question is to complete the sentence "The participants need. . . ."

4. *When?* Answering this question establishes the time frame (available time). This question invites serious consideration of just how much can be taught in the available time.
5. *What?* Answering the question *what* determines the content of the course: the skills, knowledge, and attitudes to be taught.
6. *Where?* Answering this question determines the site where the course will be presented—for instance, what facilities are available?
7. *What for?* Answering this question identifies the achievement-based objectives.

Achievement-based objectives are stated in the form "By the end of the course participants will have to. . . ." As an example, "By the end of the three-hour workshop participants will have reviewed selected theories of adult learning."

When writing achievement-based objectives, you use verbs that can be quantified, verified, and completed. Use verbs such as *practiced, designed, analyzed, selected, set in prior-ity order, distinguished between, reviewed, written, outlined, performed,* and *examined.*

Note that the content (the *what*) and the objectives are closely linked. Achievement-based objectives are what the learners will do (learning tasks) with the content in order to learn it.

Learning Task 3: Comparing Outcomes and Achievement-Based Objectives

Task 3A: Examine the one outcome and four achievement-based objectives of this unit. Indicate how learning outcomes relate to achievement-based objectives.

• Outcome: once you have worked through this unit, you will be able to use the seven steps of planning to design learning events.

- Achievement-based objectives: By the end of this unit, you will have:

  Examined a specific approach to designing adult learning, the seven steps of planning
  Compared this set of planning steps with others
  Identified the connections between learning outcomes and achievement-based objectives
  Designed part of a learning session using achievement-based objectives

Task 3B: Select any outcome you are working with in your own context. Design achievement-based objectives (*what for?*) to show what learners do with the content (*what*) to reach that outcome.

Outcome:	*Achievement-Based Objectives*
_____	_____
	_____
	_____
	_____

Learning Task 4: Designing with the Seven Steps

Take the situation you named in learning task 1. Use the seven steps of planning to name the participants and leaders (*who*), the situation (*why*), the site (*where*), and the time frame (*when*). Design at least two content pieces (*what*), two parallel achievement-based objectives (*what for*), and two learning tasks (*how*).

Congratulations! You have completed the workbook section of Unit One!

Appendix C
Technical Guide for Designing and Using Learning Tasks

Learning Task

A learning task is an open question put to a small group of people who have all the resources they need to respond.

1. Use open questions in designing learning tasks.

2. Use tough, quantitative, productive verbs.

3. Favor implied open questions, such as, "Name the best . . ." or "Describe . . ." or "Design. . . ."

4. Recognize a closed question and its implication.

Time, Time, and Time

1. Set a time short enough to keep energy up, but long enough for learning to take place.

2. In a group setting, invite feedback on the time frame ("Where are you now?").

3. Set end times ("We'll share our products at 3:00").

4. Be flexible ("In five more minutes, we'll share . . .").

5. Do not put times on all the tasks; use a large time framework.

Set Learning Tasks Clearly

1. Read the task as it is in the program.

2. Ask "Is the task clear?"

3. When invited, respond to questions for clarification, and then leave; the *learners* do the task.

4. Model the task when necessary, but be aware that such modeling narrows their choices.

5. Refuse to use such phrases as "I want you to . . ." or "I will give you more time."

Affirm Their Responses

1. Lavish affirmation creates access to energy; it takes energy to learn.

2. Affirm their effort, if not their product.

3. Affirmation is always authentic.

4. There is no such thing as too much affirmation in a learning situation.

Use Visuals and Audio Support

1. You cannot write too large on a chart.

2. Don't write on a chart anything you will not use.

3. Don't do anything that learners themselves can do.

4. For colors, choose black, brown, dark blue, dark green, or purple—never pink or yellow.

Lectures

Lectures are folded into a learning task.

1. Don't tell what you can ask, and don't ask if you know the answer; tell, in dialogue.

2. Ask yourself, *Whose voice do I hear in the learning situation?*

3. Listen to learners who take time to think before they speak (introverts).

4. Small-group work is always shared in the large group, even if there's only time for a sample.

5. Set the learning task before the lecture (input), or video, or audio, or reading, begins.

6. Invite clarifying questions prior to implementation work.

7. Lectures also need to reflect the cognitive, affective, and psychomotor aspects of learning.

Creativity

Creative learning tasks develop creativity.

1. Go for it! Use creative and imaginative learning tasks where appropriate. Break the boundaries.

2. Music, art, dance, drawings, food, sculpture . . . what can you use in your learning task?

3. In this approach, the only unforgivable sin is to trivialize.

4. There are no "little warm-ups." A warm-up is a learning task at the beginning of a set.

5. Every learning task needs some cognitive, some affective, and some psychomotor work.

Leading Learning Tasks

1. Sit still, keep quiet, and pay attention.

2. Set the task, set the time.

3. When learners are sharing, paraphrase, echo, and affirm.

4. Connect one group's learning with another's.

5. Tell what you are learning in the process.

The Program

1. Stick to the program.

2. Describe the whole program at the beginning of a session.

3. No program needs defending.

4. Change the program only after conferring with colleagues.

5. Let learners know where they are on the whole journey.

Resistance

1. Welcome resistance that shows learners are conscious of tough tasks.

2. Sometimes it's a good idea to talk to a resistant individual alone.

3. Stick to the program.

4. Work on; resistance is best met by successful learning.

5. Offer your service as a resource, not as a helper; don't do anything for a learner that he or she can do.

Preparation

1. Devote three hours of preparation to every hour of learning.

2. A dry run or rehearsal of all tasks is necessary.

3. Who's doing what? Be sure you know who in your teaching team has what responsibility.

4. Check the video, VCR, tape recorder, mike, etc.—three times.

5. Read the learning task as it is written; do not paraphrase.

6. Check the room before the course (table arrangements, easels, pens, lighting).

7. Be there at least one hour prior to the starting time.

Documentation

1. Every session is documented: the content, objectives, learning tasks, and products.

2. A record of the session is made, dated, and delivered to the client or the learners.

3. Keep all documentation for three years, filed by client or group served.

4. For our purposes, a learning session that is not documented did not take place.

Titles

1. Every course, session, and workshop has a title.

2. Every learning task has a title, such as, "Verdi Learning Task 1," or "Who Where When."

3. The document or report bears the same title as the course.

References

References Cited in This Text

Belenky, M., and others. *Women's Ways of Knowing*. New York, Basic Books, 1986.

Bloom, B. *Taxonomy of Educational Objectives*. Chicago: University of Chicago Press, 1956.

Briggs Myers, I., with Myers, P. B. *Gifts Differing: Understanding Personality Type*. Palo Alto, Calif.: Consulting Psychologists Press, 1980.

Bryson, J. *Strategic Planning for Public and Nonprofit Organizations*. San Francisco: Jossey-Bass, 1988.

Burrow, J. "On Adult Learning." (Internet course.) Raleigh: North Carolina State University, 1998.

Cabral, A. *Unity and Struggle*. New York: Monthly Review Press, 1979.

Campbell, J. *The Power of Myth*. New York: Doubleday, 1988.

Farquharson, A. *Teaching in Practice*. San Francisco: Jossey-Bass, 1995.

Fogarty, R. *Problem Based Learning and Other Curriculum Models for the Multiple Intelligences Classroom*. Arlington Heights, Va.: IRI/Skylight Training and Publishing, 1997.

Freire, P. *Pedagogy of the Oppressed*. New York: Continuum, 1993.

Gravett, S., and Henning, E. "Teaching As Dialogic Mediation: Learning Centered View of Higher Education." *South African Journal of Higher Education*, Spring 1998.

Gravett, S., and Vella, J. *Facilitating Adult Learning: A Distance Education Module*. (B.Ed. program.) Johannesburg, South Africa: Rand Afrikaans University, 1999.

Johnson, D. W., and Johnson, F. *Joining Together*. Upper Saddle River, N.J.: Prentice Hall, 1991.

Jung, C. G. *Psychological Types*. Princeton, N.J.: Princeton University Press, 1971.

Oliver, D. W., with Waldron Gershman, K. *Education, Modernity, and Fractured Meaning: Toward a Process Theory of Teaching and Learning*. Albany: SUNY Press, 1989.

Paloff, R., and Pratt, K. *Building Learning Communities in Cyberspace*. San Francisco: Jossey-Bass, 1999.

Phillips-Matz, M. J. *Verdi: A Biography*. Oxford: Oxford University Press, 1993.

Piskurich, G. *Self-Directed Learning: A Practical Guide to Design, Development, and Implementation*. San Francisco: Jossey-Bass, 1993.

Senge, P. M. *The Fifth Discipline: The Art and Practice of the Learning Organization*. New York, Doubleday/Currency, 1990.

Shor, I. *Empowering Education: Critical Teaching for Social Change*. Chicago: University of Chicago Press, 1992.

Steele, S. M. "The Evaluation of Adult and Continuing Education." In S. Merriam and P. Cunningham (eds.), *Handbook of Adult and Continuing Education*. San Francisco: Jossey-Bass, 1989.

Vella, J. *Learning to Listen, Learning to Teach: The Power of Dialogue in Educating Adults*. San Francisco: Jossey-Bass, 1994a.

Vella, J. "Training Trainers in the Principles and Practices of Popular Education." *Convergence*, 1994b, *27*(1), 27–36.

Vella, J. *Training Through Dialogue*. San Francisco: Jossey-Bass, 1995.

Vella, J., Berardinelli, P., and Burrow, J. *How Do They Know They Know: Evaluating Adult Learning*. San Francisco: Jossey-Bass, 1998.

Vella, J., and Uccellani, V. *Learning to Listen to Mothers*. Washington, D.C.: Academy for Educational Development, 1993.

Wheatley, M. *Leadership and the New Science*. (Rev. ed.) San Francisco: Berrett-Koehler, 1999.

Wlodkowski, R. J., and Ginsberg, M. B. *Diversity and Motivation: Culturally Responsive Teaching*. San Francisco: Jossey-Bass, 1996.

Sources for Further Learning

Arnold, R. *Educating for a Change*. Toronto: Between the Lines, and Doris Marshall Institute for Education and Action, 1991.

Bakhtin, M. "Discourse in the Novel." In M. Holquist (ed.), *The Dialogic Imagination: Four Essays by Mikhail Bakhtin*. University of Texas Slavic Series no. 1. Austin: University of Texas Press, 1981.

Beamish, J., and Vella, J. *Developing Health Journalists*. Research Triangle Park, N.C.: Family Health International, 1993.

Brookfield, S. *Self-Directed Learning: From Theory to Practice*. New Directions for Continuing Education, no. 25. San Francisco: Jossey-Bass, 1985.

Brookfield, S. *Understanding and Facilitating Adult Learning: A Comprehensive Analysis of Principles and Effective Practices*. San Francisco: Jossey-Bass, 1986.

Brownsword, A. E. *It Takes All Types*. San Anselmo Calif.: Baytree, 1987.

Caine, R. N., and Caine, G. *Making Connections: Teaching and the Human Brain*. Alexandria: Virginia Association for Supervision and Curriculum Development, 1991.

Candy, P. C. *Self-Direction for Lifelong Learning: A Comprehensive Guide to Theory and Practice*. San Francisco: Jossey-Bass, 1991.

Cranton, P. *Understanding and Promoting Transformative Learning: A Guide for Educators of Adults*. San Francisco: Jossey-Bass, 1994.

Freire, P. *Cultural Action for Freedom*. Monograph Series no. 1. Cambridge, Mass.: Harvard Educational Review, 1975.

Freire, P., and Faundez, A. *Learning to Question. A Pedagogy of Liberation*. New York: Continuum, 1989.

Hope, A., and Timmel, S. *Training for Transformation*. Gweru, Zimbabwe: Mambo Press, 1989.

Horton, M., and Freire, P. *We Make the Road by Walking*. Philadelphia: Temple University Press, 1990.

James, M., and Jongeward, D. *Born to Win*. Reading, Mass.: Addison-Wesley, 1971.

Kindervatter, S. *Nonformal Education as an Empowering Process*. Amherst: Center for International Education, University of Massachusetts, 1979.

Kindervatter, S. *Women Working Together for Personal, Economic, and Community Development.* Washington, D.C.: OEF International, 1987.

Knowles, M., and Associates. *Andragogy in Action: Applying Modern Principles of Adult Learning.* San Francisco: Jossey-Bass, 1984.

Meyers, C., and Jones, T. *Promoting Active Learning.* San Francisco: Jossey-Bass, 1993.

Palmer, P. *The Courage to Teach.* San Francisco: Jossey-Bass, 1998.

Schwarz, R. M. *The Skilled Facilitator.* San Francisco: Jossey-Bass, 1994.

Shor, I., and Freire, P. "What Is the 'Dialogical Method' of Teaching?" *Journal of Education,* 1987, *168*(3), 11–31.

Sousa, D. *How the Brain Learns.* Reston, Va.: National Association of Secondary School Principals, 1995.

Srinivasan, L. *Options for Educators. Monograph for Decision Makers on Alternative Participatory Strategies.* New York: PACT/CDS, 1992.

Svendsen, D., and Wijellitakane, S. *Navamaga.* New York: WomenInk, 1986.

Vella, J. *Learning to Listen.* Amherst: Center for International Education, University of Massachusetts, 1979.

Vella, J. *Learning to Teach.* Westport, Conn.: Save the Children, 1989.

Vella, J. *Visual Aids for Nonformal Education.* Amherst: Center for International Education, University of Massachusetts, 1979.

Index